W9-AEI-165

# MEDIAEVAL DRAMA IN CHESTER

# THE ALEXANDER LECTURESHIP

THE ALEXANDER LECTURESHIP was founded in honour of Professor W. J. Alexander, who held the Chair of English at University College from 1889 to 1926. Each year the Lectureship brings to the University a distinguished scholar or critic to give a course of lectures on a subject related to English Literature.

# MEDIAEVAL DRAMA

# IN CHESTER

## F. M. SALTER

*University of Toronto Press*

TYPOGRAPHY AND DECORATIONS BY ANTJE LINGNER

# THE ALEXANDER LECTURES

(Unless otherwise indicated the lectures have been
published by the University of Toronto Press)

1941–42    H. J. DAVIS: *Stella, a Gentlewoman of the Eighteenth Century* (Macmillan, 1942)

1942–43    H. GRANVILLE-BARKER: Coriolanus
Included in the author's *Prefaces to Shakespeare: Vol. II* (Princeton, 1947)

1943–44    F. P. WILSON: *Elizabethan and Jacobean* (Clarendon, 1945)

1944–45    F. O. MATTHIESSEN: *Henry James, the Major Phase* (Oxford, 1944)

1945–46    S. C. CHEW: *The Virtues Reconciled, an Iconographical Study* (1947)

1946–47    MARJORIE HOPE NICOLSON: *Voyages to the Moon* (Macmillan, 1948)

1947–48    G. B. HARRISON: Shakespearean Tragedy
Included in the author's *Shakespeare's Tragedies* (Routledge and Kegan Paul, 1951)

1948–49    E. M. W. TILLYARD: *Shakespeare's Problem Plays* (1949)

1949–50    E. K. BROWN: *Rhythm in the Novel* (1950)

1950–51    MALCOLM W. WALLACE: *English Character and the English Literary Tradition* (1952)

1951–52    R. S. CRANE: *The Languages of Criticism and the Structure of Poetry* (1953)

1952–53    No lectures given.

1953–54    F. M. SALTER: *Mediaeval Drama in Chester* (1955)

# PREFACE

EDIAEVAL DRAMA IN CHESTER" may seem an inaccurate title for lectures which actually reach the seventeenth century; but it is the type of drama, rather than the period, that is in question.

These lectures represent, I trust, only a part of my "late harvest"—if I may use the title of one of the books of a Canadian professor by me deeply beloved, Archibald MacMechan. He was to me what his friend, W. J. Alexander, must also have been to many—a beginning. When I first became interested in mediaeval drama, however, I did so under the tutelage of John Matthews Manly who had, of all the men I have personally known, the soundest and most brilliant intellect. He was the soul of kindness, as Miss Rickert, his long associate, was an infinitude of charm and inspiration. Through these persons, and through C. R. Baskervill whose memory was encyclopaedic and amazing, and whose slow and genial smile it was a joy to provoke, I once walked—in Rupert Brooke's fine phrase—"proudly friended." And through them all in their variety of still-living influence, I can understand what Professor Alexander must have meant to his colleagues at Toronto and to generations of students.

With these names I should like to associate that of Sir W. W. Greg. He represents to me, and long has done, not only exact and far-reaching and voluminous scholarship, and not only hospitality and a helping hand to the stranger within the gates, but Magnanimity, the last and greatest of the Twelve Moral Virtues.

Over the many years, I have received courtesies and help

from many sources: from the officials and staff of the British
Museum and the Bodleian, of the National Library of Wales
and Cambridge University Library, from the civic and ecclesiastical officers of Chester and from the Stewards of the many surviving Chester Gilds. The University of Alberta granted me some
years ago a most generous sabbatical year; and from the John
Simon Guggenheim Memorial Foundation, the Henry E. Huntington Library, and the British Council I have received not only
kindness and encouragement, but even the "wherwith to sco-
leye."

Many of those persons who have assisted me have gone beyond the reach of my voice, for the years take their inevitable
toll. It will perhaps not seem ungallant if I let two names stand
as symbols of the many to whom I am indebted: the names of
Maud Sellers and Dorothy I. Hamilton.

Maud Sellers must have been one of the earliest women scholars
of the modern age—and a splendid scholar she was. I knew her
when she was very old and dedicating her energies to the Mer-
chant Adventurers Hall of York. Whatever our relationship
meant to her, to me it was love at first sight—and at last sight.
She was greatly concerned that I should not work too hard!
and effectively prevented my doing so with tales I would give
my two ears to hear again. With the keenest and most joyous
eagerness she helped me ransack the records of York for information about Mystery Plays.

Miss Hamilton is Reference Librarian at the University of
Alberta; and for selfless devotion to readers worthy and un-
worthy, she has no equal. I think if she had to tear a book from
the hug of a grizzly bear for a reader, she would do it quite
calmly and with no fuss—and with no desire for thanks. My
debt to her is great indeed, and she symbolizes by no means the
smallest item in a great account.

With all the help and encouragement it is, alas, no Parian

marble that I bring to the inspiring monument which, year by year, the University of Toronto is building to the memory of their own beloved professor—but only a piece of field-stone retrieved by a prairie boy. Handled lovingly enough and treasured long, as it has been, it may serve as part of the interior rubble of a great work.

And finally, to President Sidney E. Smith of the University of Toronto, the most winsome of men; to F. C. A. Jeanneret, Principal of University College, whom I knew for a brief moment long ago at Chicago, retaining always a memory of his warm geniality; and to Professor A. S. P. Woodhouse, the Dean of English studies in Canada, whom to have known for only a few years is certainly better than not to have known him at all; to these and to many others at Toronto I must express my gratitude for hospitality overwhelming and heart-warming. But most of all, I must thank them for giving me an opportunity—and a deadline—to clothe in comely print ideas too long left unrecorded.

F. M. S.

*The University of Alberta*
*June, 1954*

# CONTENTS

# MEDIAEVAL DRAMA IN CHESTER

HREE TRIBUTARY STREAMS flow into the great river of Elizabethan drama. All of these in some degree, however slight, can be illustrated from the records of the city of Chester.

It will be convenient, in this first lecture, to summarize the story of the birth of drama in the Western world, its nurture and growth in England down to the days of the first professional secular theatre; and then to indicate how that story finds documentation in Chester.

The earliest or most ancient stream of English drama flows out of folk materials. These materials are as old as the various tribes whose stock eventually united to people the British Isles. St. George himself, if indeed he was not actually that legendary Perseus who slew the sea-monster, is typical of this material in the uncertainty that surrounds his story and in the geographical diffusion of his exploits. Cynics have asserted that no such monster as the dragon ever existed—as if we had not in our own day seen it slain afresh, the terror that flieth by night breathing fire and Götterdämmerung. Moreover, I have myself seen the very spot where St. George slew the dragon. The place is still there as a perennial testimonial and reproof to disbelievers. Indeed, I have seen three places where he slew it, and therefore retain a threefold conviction that the legend represents incontrovertible fact. Further evidence of the actual historical existence of St. George—whom some scoffers call St. George of Cappadocia, and not St. George of England—may be found in the Mummers' plays of which he is, with amazing consistency, always the hero, or one of the heroes. In these St. George, living longer than

3

Methuselah, is contemporary with King Alfred, Oliver Cromwell, and King William of blessed memory, not to mention Old
King Cole and Beelzebub. We may conclude, but not without
due scholarly caution, that historical elements are somewhat
confused in the mummers' plays. The same point can be made
of all folk materials which—if an Irish bull may express it—
suffer a sea-change before they find their way into the great
river of drama.

But still I run before my horse to market. What is a mummers' play? Hardy gives a good account of one in *The Return
of the Native*. It is hardly more than a crude disguising. Children or country lads costume themselves to represent St. George,
Old King Cole, Captain Slasher, the Turkish Champion, and
similar characters. They enter a house and perform in the
kitchen or hall. Each has a few verses in which to identify himself. Generally there is a fight in which all the characters are
killed. Their mutual massacre makes necessary the entrance of
"Mr. Dr. Ball" who forces huge pills down their throats, where-
upon they all come to, pass the hat, and make for the next house.
The entertainment may be spiced with morris dancing or jigs;
and the mummers' play belongs to such seasons as Christmas
and Hallowe'en.

Such simple dramatics as these may originate in pre-Christian
peregrinations and games, in pagan fertility rites, heathen customs at the beginning of winter or its end, or in ceremonies to
banish evil spirits from the fields. The processional element is
regular in them. And as the Church took over ancient festivals
and shrines and adapted them to Christian purposes, there seems
to have been a perennial recoil of paganism upon the Church
itself, which may be seen in the Feast of Fools, the Boy Bishop,
and the wilder ceremonies of the Christmas season. The net result of this age-old interaction between Christianity and paganism is that it is difficult to find in folk materials clear lines of
descent from their origin.

Like St. George of the mummers' plays, Robin Hood became, somewhat later, the centre of a whole cluster of folk drama— and the professional stage has seen Robin Hood not once or twice, but many times, in its four-century history. It is quite likely that the surviving mummers' plays also have given rise to, or are descended from, performances once much more substantial and amusing, for there are records of St. George plays or shows performed before Edward III in 1348, at Coventry in 1474, and at Bassingbourne in 1511.[1] But it is fair to say that the folk-material stream (which is by no means fully represented by St. George and Robin Hood), although it is the most ancient tributary, sends the thinnest trickle into the flood of modern drama. Or perhaps it contributes an influence pervasive but difficult to isolate, analyse, or estimate, for the courtly masque, later attractive to the pens of Ben Jonson and John Milton, is at least first cousin to the mumming play;[2] and it need hardly be proved that the masque with its spectacular features and its elaborate stage scenery and machines made a great contribution to the physical stage. The folk influence upon our drama, in a word, is Protean and Antæan: elusive in form and shape, and difficult to pin down. *may exist — he's not sure*

The second stream of drama is more immediately religious in origin and more substantial in contribution. To understand it properly, we must return to a day when comparatively few men and women could read or write, and when the mediaeval Church, the greatest teacher the world has known, faced the problem of propagating the faith. For faith is indispensable if our souls are to be saved: it is faith that makes us whole. The difficulty was that the things in which men and women had to believe were things contrary to all the normal experience of mankind. They must, first of all, believe that a Man was born of a Virgin; and, further, they must believe that that Man was crucified, dead, and buried, yet the third day He rose again. It was to be expected that the great ceremonials of the Christian year would fall at Christmas and Easter to celebrate that birth and that death and resurrection in which men must believe, or perish.

In schools of education and normal schools prospective teachers are taught the value of drill, or constant repetition; and they are taught to appeal, if possible, to more than one of the senses of their pupils. Need one mention the impressive repetitions of the Mass? But the Church found the means of appealing not to one or two of the senses, but to all five! There is appeal to the sense of touch in the carvings, in the hand of the priest on the head of the penitent, and in the very feel of the house of God. There is appeal to the sense of smell in the incense, the fragrance of holiness. Sight is appealed to in the splendour of stained glass and paintings and statuary, in the meaningful robes, processional, and genuflections; and the sense of hearing is filled with the magnificent chanting of the Mass and with those great hymns, like *Dies Irae* and *Te Deum*, which have never lost their profound impressiveness. Finally, at the very moment of greatest drama, the sense of taste is touched, "Take, eat: this is My body. . . . This is My blood."

I would not at all suggest that the Mass was developed in any such designing fashion as this bare account may suggest; what I do mean is that the Church could gladly adopt any means whereby faith might grow in the multitude; and in the ninth century, long after the professional stage of ancient Rome had disappeared, small insertions of actual drama appeared in churches all over Europe within those services which themselves—in the processionals, in the symbolism of priestly vestments, in the imitative peregrination of the Stations of the Cross, and in all the rites and ceremonial—had strong elements of the dramatic.[3] These insertions are called Tropes.

All that is needed is that on Easter morning after the Third Responsory, a choir boy dressed in white and carrying a palm, the symbol of a heavenly messenger, should seat himself before the High Altar. From the choir three persons, dressed to represent the three Mary's, approach him. He asks, "Whom seek ye in the sepulchre, O followers of Christ?" They answer, "We seek Jesus of Nazareth who was crucified, O celestial one." The angel replies, "He is not here, but risen, as He foretold. Go, announce that He is risen from the dead." That is all; the actors resume their places in the choir, and the music and magnificence of the service flow on around this little island.

This bit of representation was undoubtedly popular and moving. Being so, it was naturally enlarged. The three Mary's, going away, meet Peter and John and tell them the great news. These run toward the Tomb; but John, being younger, gets there first. He stands aside, and Peter looks into the Tomb, takes up the cloths in which the Cross, representing the body of Christ, had been wrapped on Good Friday, and displays them to the congregation. Other incidents are added until the story of the Passion is fully developed. When the trope has been thus enlarged, we call it a Liturgical play.[4] And, as evidence of the inextricable mixture of elements and ideas from both Germanic and Christian origins, it has been argued that the whole liturgical play itself, like the mummers' plays, is derived from pre-Christian pagan rites.[5]

In time, the liturgical play becomes too extended to be contained as a mere episode within the Mass; and the next question is whether it is not worthy of separate production in its own right. At any rate, the liturgical plays were separately produced, and various parts of the church were spotted for various scenes: for the scene before Herod, the scene before the High Priests, the scene of Gethsemane—and a pedestal was even found for the cock which crew when Peter denied our Lord. But there is one curious thing, seeing that the intent of the religious authorities was to instruct; and this is that the tropes and liturgical plays, like the Mass itself, continued to be produced in Latin, which was certainly not understood by the common people. No doubt there were the same arguments about translation as we have heard regarding grand opera, with the additional consideration that the vernacular would have seemed incongruous within a Latin ritual, even though occasional vernacular words do appear. As long as the drift was understood, perhaps the sonorous Latin was more impressive.

Just here, seeing that the tradition of Shakespeare's "bare stage" is one which, popularly, dies hard or not at all, it may be added that the liturgical plays developed quite elaborate staging devices within the church as early as the thirteenth century.[6] But the church was never designed as a theatre; and performances within it must always have been difficult for the whole audience to see. The reasonable thing to do was to move the liturgical play outside to the great west door and place it on stands. That was done.

With the growth of the play, two things would immediately come into sharp focus. The first is the expense of production; the second is the necessity of numerous actors. Both must have strained the resources of the Church; and the inevitable solution was found in the mediaeval craft gild and its place in the structure of mediaeval society.

It is often forgotten that the craft gild was a semi-religious organization. Every craft had its patron saint; and it maintained its own chapel, hospital, or shrine within the church. In other respects also it differed from the modern trade union. It existed largely to protect the public from poor goods and shoddy workmanship; and the aldermen annually elected by the gilds to manage their affairs joined together as an inter-gild body which became the city council. From their members they elected the Mayor of the city. In some respects the gilds resembled more an organization of employers than a union of workmen—but, of course, employers on a modest scale.[7] Every gild looked after its own members, maintaining the sick and unfortunate, the widows and orphans, and taking care of the interests, both economic and spiritual, of its members. It was perfectly natural that the Church should turn to the craft gilds for assistance in producing the religious play, and that the gilds should accept an opportunity for advertising.

With this change, two things came about. Being composed of business men, the gilds naturally would desire a definite and clearly understood obligation. Therefore the single play was broken up into pieces which could be assigned to individual crafts. Secondly, the large numbers of actors now required and supplied by the craft gilds could not speak Latin. Therefore the plays began to appear in the vernacular.[8]

The French word *mystère* (modern *métier*) signified a craft; and the word *mystery* as signifying a craft or occupation is common in English as early as 1375. When the religious plays have been taken over by the mystery or craft gilds, they are called Mystery plays.[9] The process of growth and division of the plays themselves went on. At first, there would be a joining up of the events of the Christian year: Christmas and Easter, the birth of our Lord and His crucifixion and resurrection; but as time went on, the basic scheme was enlarged to take in the whole story of the Bible and the Apocrypha from Adam to Antichrist, the whole story of man from Genesis to Judgment Day. At York there were no fewer than forty-eight individual plays; at Chester, twenty-six.

Another logical development out of the liturgical play is the Miracle play. After all, the subjects of miracle plays are, initially, equally Biblical or religious in character; and a religious gild might well perform within the church the story of the life and miracles of a saint. Indeed, Karl Young gives examples of *liturgical* plays of the Raising of Lazarus and the Conversion of St. Paul,[10] and we have references to others in the twelfth century apparently designed to celebrate saints' days. Such plays as these, produced by religious gilds, could have moved out from within the church even earlier than the cyclic plays of the craft gilds. In England we have the names of and references to many such miracle plays, but only three have survived: *The Croxton Play of the Sacrament, The Play of Mary Magdalene,* and *The Conversion of St. Paul.*

A development not quite so logical, not quite so predictable, is the Morality play. This is a play in which all the characters are abstractions. Thus in the play of *Mankind,* the characters are: Mankind, Mercy, Mischief, New-Guise, Now-a-days, Nought, and Titivillus. These plays indulged in the spectacular. For example, in *The Castle of Perseverance* the forces of evil are driven off from the castle by the forces of good—and the ammunition hurled from the battlements consists of showers of red roses! One of these plays, *Everyman,* is still frequently performed by church groups; indeed, it could be argued that *Everyman* has seen more productions than any play of Shakespeare's.

Exactly how the morality originated nobody knows.[11] It would seem to have been begotten upon religious drama—mystery and miracle—by mediaeval preaching. As early as the twelfth century individual abstract figures appear in the *Antichristus* play;[12] and "Dethe, Goddys masangere" appears in the *Ludus Coventriae,* a late imitation of the craft cycle. Further evidence of the intrusion of abstract characters into drama may be seen in the miracle play of *Mary Magdalene* in which Angelus and Diabolus, representing the powers of good and evil, struggle for the soul of Mary. Clear proof of the fertility of the mediaeval sermon may be seen in the Paternoster plays. Our ancestors believed that each clause of the Lord's Prayer, or Paternoster, held specific saving grace against one of the deadly sins; and the Paternoster play of Beverley, which has not come down to us, had a pageant for each of the seven deadly sins. It may well be true, as Chambers has suggested,[13] that the Paternoster plays are early moralities.

One point I should like to make is that in my opinion the morality, like all the religious drama of England, is of folk origin, just as the ballads are, except that in this case the folk are members of religious orders and their parishioners. When the morality became, in its latest days, a vehicle of conscious literary men, just as the ballad did, the picture may have been different; but in the beginning it was purely instructional, a histrionic sermon, nothing more.[14]

There is, however, a possible relationship between the morality and the Royal Entry, just as there is a possible relationship between the mumming play and the courtly masque; and in both cases I would give priority in time to the poor relation across the tracks. The royal entry was simply an elaborate show designed to welcome royal persons at the gates of a city. Spectacular effects were contrived and symbolical figures pronounced laudatory speeches. John Lydgate is said to have written verses for shows of the royal entry type;[15] and it is significant that John Skelton and Sir David Lyndsay, the only known authors of moralities—and these very late in the history of the genre—were both court poets. The possible relationship of the two genres is to be seen in the sumptuous staging devices used by both.

The moralities tended to excessive length. Sir David Lyndsay's *Satyre of the Thrie Estaitis* required three days for full performance. Solid morality, also, is hard to take. For relief, comic Interludes were brought in. These were simply bits of farce or nonsense; but they developed, especially in the hands of John Heywood in the early sixteenth century, into something rather like the modern one-act play. They could be used not only to liven up the tedious moralities, but also independently as entertainment at the interminable banquets of our ancestors in a setting rather more courtly than that of the mystery plays.

Now, although I have spoken of interludes and moralities as growing out of mystery plays and miracles, as these in turn grew out of liturgical drama and tropes, the phoenix did not need in each case to die before a new phoenix could be born. Actually, the tropes continued from the end of the ninth century to the third quarter of the sixteenth when they were banned at the Council of Trent (1545–63); the liturgical plays lasted from about the tenth century to the sixteenth, the thirteenth century being the period of their greatest growth and diffusion; the mystery plays covered the period from about 1375 to 1575; the miracles a slightly earlier period, with an earlier disappearance; the moralities from about 1400, in their full development, until they merged in professional secular drama; and the interludes, similarly merging in the end, from about 1475 onwards.[16] I have dated the mysteries as beginning about 1375. This date is at variance with the dates given by Chambers and other authorities who believe that they began before 1300;[17] but in the next lecture I shall offer evidence to suggest that a later date is more likely.

I left the mystery play being performed upon stands at the great west door of the church; but it made a further significant contribution to professional secular drama. When the crowds coming to see the plays became too large to be accommodated, our logical ancestors split them into smaller groups. For this purpose they put the stage on wheels. The play could now be performed in Chester, for example, before one group at the gates of St. Werburgh's Abbey, before another group at the High Cross, then at the Castle, and finally by the river on the extensive open space called the Roodee.

Once the stage has been placed upon wheels, it can be carried far and wide; and there is evidence of strolling players during the fifteenth century. It has often been pointed out that the Prologue of the vexillatores in *The Castle of Perseverance*, generally dated 1425, implies that the performers of this morality moved from town to town. If that play could be moved, requiring as it does elaborate arrangements including a moat or ditch dug all round the playing place, it is the more likely that Robin Hood plays and interludes were acted by strolling players. Some of these, of course, could be produced anywhere, in any hall or open place; but others must have needed some properties. By the early sixteenth century, at any rate, strolling players are numerous.[18]

Now the most essential practical necessity of the professional theatre is a gate. As long as the actors must pass a hat for gratuities, only the poorest living can be collected, for at the first sign of the hat, the crowd melts away. The stage on wheels in time answered that difficulty, and permitted the professional theatre to be born.

The typical inn of mediaeval times was a square building surrounding an inner court into which coaches could drive through a built-over gateway. The inn, really, was a modest adaptation of the ancient castle. Verandahs on the inner or courtyard side led to the rooms, and stairways connected various levels. Once the stage has become a wheeled vehicle, all that is necessary is to set it across the inner side of the gateway and advertise the play. Nobody can get in without paying, and professional drama becomes possible. When the Burbages built their first theatre, they adapted precisely this design; and the great Globe which saw the first performance of so many of Shakespeare's plays was equally open to the sky except—as in the inn itself—over the stage and over the verandahs where the higher-paying customers sat while the *hoi polloi* stood in the courtyard.

Two of the streams, then, which flow into Elizabethan drama

are the folk stream and the religious stream with its variety of forms. The latest stream in time is that of classical drama.[19] Theatre performances of Roman drama had disappeared from the world in the sixth century;[20] but the texts remained. That classical drama ever contributed its fruitful influence to the modern stage is due primarily to that great upheaval which we call the Reformation.

It is difficult in modern times to realize the domination which the mediaeval Church exerted over all human life. Something of the picture we see in Chaucer, a full third of whose pilgrims are in some way connected with the Church. Moreover, we owe the basic idea of *The Canterbury Tales* to the many pilgrimages to holy shrines, which served a purpose then perhaps even nobler than those served now by our conventions of scholars, business men, and old soldiers. There was no other institution than the Church to which one might leave by will money or lands, for, with few exceptions, the Church was the only eleemosynary organization, the only hospital, the only home for the aged, the only art gallery, the only library, the only publisher—and the Church maintained the only schools. Consequently, when Henry VIII disestablished the Church, the problem of education leaped immediately into the foreground; and most of the great public schools of England—Eton, Harrow, Charterhouse, etc.—were founded, or founded anew, at that time.

With the establishment of schools no longer conducted under the unquestionable authority of the Church, a widespread new interest in education sprang up; and one of the novel methods of teaching brought into service at that time was the performance by children of the Latin plays they studied. It is only a step to having them write plays in Latin—and this tradition is still followed at Westminster School where annually members of Parliament, like Churchill and Attlee, are invited to hear themselves abused in Latin. What is now happening, to return to the sixteenth century, is that young men from the schools are going to the universities with some familiarity with Latin drama as a stage vehicle, and especially with the popular comedies of Plautus and Terence. We may expect similar plays in English; and *Ralph Roister Doister* and *Gammer Gurton's Nedle*, written for school dramatics, soon answer the expectation.

All that is now needed is a professional group of actors, for the three streams of dramatic influence are flowing together, and the stage with gate attached is ready. As a consequence, in the 1570's, while Shakespeare is still a boy in Stratford, professional secular drama is born; for the professional group of actors is actually, and has long been, in being. They appear in the households of various lords and princes, and in the household of the king himself as early as the time of Henry VII, usually labelled in the accounts as "My Lord's players of interludes." The roads also are full of strolling entertainers, often lumped in repressive enactments with "sturdy beggars." But the time is coming when, in spite of the hostility of Puritans and others, a man will be able to make a living as an actor, free of beggary and independent of patronage. Nay, he will even be able, like Shakespeare, to bear the arms of a gentleman; and, like Alleyn, to endow colleges. To challenge his quality, moreover, he will have the learning and genius of Jonson, and Marlowe's mighty line.

This account of the development of drama in England has had to be brief, scanty, and compressed—with, of course, a corresponding distortion of emphasis and inevitable inexactness. It is now time to make good the claim that the history of drama can be documented from the records of the city of Chester.

It would be too much to expect that every one of the many forms of drama could be illustrated from the records of any one town, considering the hazards all records are heir to within even a single generation. Further, most of the surviving Chester records belong to the sixteenth century, coming at the very end of the long period with which we are concerned. Nevertheless, they do yield some interesting glimpses of our drama in its formative days.

First the religious drama. No tropes have come down to us from Chester, and no manuscripts of liturgical plays. But there do exist in Harley MS. 2177, copies of Churchwardens' accounts from various churches in Chester made by Randle Holme II in 1650. The original accounts seem to have disappeared. Altogether, there were four indefatigable antiquaries by this name: Randle Holme the First, Second, Third, and Fourth; and the Harley MSS. in the British Museum include many of their multitudinous collections.

At an early stage in the development of the liturgical play, as we have seen, it was customary to place a cross bound in burial cloths in a sepulchre before the High Altar on Good Friday. On Easter morning, after the angel has announced the Resurrection of our Lord and the Mary's have repeated this glad tidings to Peter and John, these disciples run to the Tomb, and finding it empty, pick up the cloths left lying within and display them to the worshippers. For the Christmas play the shepherds come in at the west door of the church and follow a star high in the nave until it comes to rest above the stable where Mary and Joseph and the new-born child await them before the altar.

The following items, excerpted from Harley MS. 2177,[21] will illustrate these proceedings:

1535    rec. of m^r bomvell of the gift of his wife a fyne napkyn of Calico cloth trelyd w^th silk to couer the Crosse in y^e sepulcre

Fol. 20^v

1545–6    for pyns & thred to make the sepuclre [sic] ij^d

Fol. 21^v

1553   payd for the starr   ij$^s$

·   ·   ·   ·   ·   ·   ·   ·   ·

·   ·   ·   ·   ·   ·   ·   ·   ·

payd for paper & writtinge the senses & solens to the starr   4$^d$

·   ·   ·   ·   ·   ·   ·   ·   ·

·   ·   ·   ·   ·   ·   ·   ·   ·

to the clarke for wachinge the sepulcre   ix$^d$          Fol. 23$^r$

1556–7   for wachinge the sepulcre one night to the clarke iij d. & after in berrage ij d. for takinge downe the clothes about the sepulcar   ij$^d$

for hollyns to make the hollyn agaynst christmas & sences vnto the starr w$^{th}$ a chales of paper   8$^d$

for cressets to sett in candles & makinge balls to the sences   1$^d$

for wyryd candles to the hollyn   xv$^d$

for weshinge 2 sirpls & thrid to sow on the fannonce ix$^d$ ob.

for nayles & pynns at seueral tymes for the sepulcar & alter clothes, etc.

·   ·   ·   ·   ·   ·   ·   ·   ·

·   ·   ·   ·   ·   ·   ·   ·   ·

for settinge vp & takinge downe the sepulcar   4$^d$

wachinge the scpulcar 2 nights   4$^d$

payd a wright for a frame for lightes vnto thc sepulcre   4$^d$
                                                          Fol. 25$^r$

1558   for wyer candles wax candles etc. scouring candlesticks wachinge the sepulcre at Ester etc. for a pully to the starr & setting it vp   4$^d$

1559   for senses for the starr   i$^d$

for wax to make tapers   18$^d$

wachinge the sepulcre at ester   viij$^d$

What "sences and solens" are, I do not know. The *New English*

*Dictionary* would permit us to take *sense* to mean a discourse. *Solens* may have a connection with solemn or solemnization. Whatever they are, the sences and solens had to be written, and it is perhaps not too wild a guess to take them to mean players' parts and songs. The Easter sepulchre and the "pully to the starr" must imply drama of some sort at both Easter and Christmas, whether trope or liturgical play. After 1559, Queen Elizabeth having come to the throne and the country being for the second time officially Protestant, these items disappear from the Churchwardens' accounts.

The most abundant records at Chester are those which concern the craft or mystery plays; but these I shall leave for later lectures. Only, it may be of interest here to question what became of all the beautiful coloured vestments of the Roman Catholic Church when the country went in for a grimmer form of Christianity. The abundance of these vestments made the costuming of mystery plays a simple matter of borrowing. When the Church of Rome disappeared, and its trappings with it, the mystery plays would become both more difficult and more costly to produce—and this impulse towards discontinuance of the mystery is one I have never seen mentioned. But, in fact, what did happen to the vestments, to say nothing of censers and chalices and all the necessary equipment of the older religion? The question is simple and obvious to ask; but I have never seen the answer, except in the Churchwardens' accounts of Holy Trinity.

First of all, let us gain some idea of what was involved. Harley MS. 2177 has a copy of an inventory "Of the Godis now beyng in Trenyte church of Chester 1532":

Impr. on chalis w^th paten [base] all gylde Cont. 13 onz.

on other chalis with paten all gyld Cont. 16 onz & halph

Itm a Sencer: Itm a cross of Coper & gylde: Itm a ringe of siluer with a white Stone in it

Itm a Cope of cloth of gould, a Cope of Red veluet

Itm a vestment of greene damask. A nowbe [alb] & stole and amysse & fermer to the same

Itm a vestment of Rede taffata with a nowbe & stole & amysse & fermer to it

Itm a vestment of Red Sarsanett with an owbe & stole & amysse & fermer to it

Itm a vestment of blew saten w<sup>th</sup> an owbe stole & amysse & fermer to it

a rede vestment for passion weeke and 2 Tennacles & one white tenacle

Itm 4 tunacles of changeable silke

a vestment of greene dorneks [i.e. from Doornik or Tournai] w<sup>th</sup> an owbe stole amysse & fermer to it

Itm an other of the same w<sup>th</sup> owbe stole amysse & fermer to it

Itm 2 Course Cops a crymson Crane color & yelow

4 vestments 2 of sylke & 2 of dorneks

Itm one white vestment for Lent-tyme

Itm 2 stoles w<sup>th</sup> a fermer of cloth of silke and gould

Itm an Alter Cloth for the high Alter of grene & tawnye

Itm 3 copes one for holye days & other for werke days

Itm an alter cloth of behound sey [beyond sea] werke & 2 curtayns for the same

Itm 5 Corpars w<sup>th</sup> Casses

Itm a baner for the crosse of grene sarsenet

Itm foure other baners for the Crosse weeke & 4 speares for the same

Itm a Couerlyd of red for the crepynge to the Crosse

Itm 3 alter clothes

Itm 6 towells of lynnynne Cloth for the lauater of the masse

Itm 2 pillow bers sowed w<sup>th</sup> black silke

Itm a vale of yelow & black

Itm an alter cloth for the hee alter for euery day

Itm a Tee w$^{th}$ 4 Cofforse belongynge to the cherche

Itm 2 chaundlers of bras

Itm a buckett of brasse for holy water

Itm a chanler of pewter for the pascall

Itm a serpls for procession dayes

    This inventory represents a sizable investment for a small parish church; and, of course, it was added to from time to time, and gifts came in like that already mentioned of a napkin to cover the Cross in the sepulchre. In 1551 while Edward VI was on the throne, the churchwardens began to dispose of equipment no longer needed. When Mary acceded in 1553, they must have felt that they had been too hasty. Another inventory of 1557 shows Holy Trinity once more well appointed for Roman Catholic services. By 1560, however, Mary having died and Elizabeth having succeeded two years earlier, the wardens are again selling Roman furnishings, as the following entries show:

1560    Church goods deliuered to M$^r$ hardware Maior the best Cope & the vestment & appurtenances also he hath a Challes in paune for 30$^s$ more to him 3 veluett quyssions [cushions]

    M$^r$ Rafe goodman receued a vestment of satayn bridges [of Bruges?] & 2 hangins of stow w$^{th}$ one fringe of silke w$^{th}$ appertenances also 2 Canopyes of sassnett & a vestment of Dornett

    Willm leche rec' a vestment & 2 tunacles of blew veluet w$^{ch}$ we sould to him for 40$^s$

    John Eton rec' a vestment of grene damaske

    Rich boydell a vestment of Chamlett

    John Shaw a vestment of white damaske

    M$^{rs}$ gyttyns 2 pillowes w$^{th}$ beres & a sheite

    M$^r$ Jones the great Candlesticks of bras    Fol. 27$^v$

1568 Memorand' 2 may 1568 hen' Hardware did account w<sup>th</sup> the parishioners of Trinity for a Cope vestment & other thinges sould by hamnett Iohnson his seruant to Io Curton of bilbow [Bilboa, Spain] for 770 royalls at vj<sup>d</sup> le Royall w<sup>ch</sup> came to 19<sup>li</sup> 5<sup>s</sup> & payd xv<sup>li</sup> vj<sup>s</sup> 8<sup>d</sup> & rested owinge the parish 3<sup>li</sup> 14<sup>s</sup> 4<sup>d</sup> vnder his hand on the same lease. Fol. 28<sup>r</sup>

1573 Mem<sup>d</sup> dauid chaloner marchant doth owe for an ould cope of Redd veluett xl<sup>s</sup> to be payd at his returne from spayne and will<sup>m</sup> pyllyn marchant is surtye Fol. 29<sup>v</sup>

In due time Henry Hardware and David Chaloner squared their accounts. Spain was still a Roman Catholic country, and a market for vestments no longer needed in England. Some of the golden and pewter vessels were simply melted down; but there are two further items in these accounts which are worth a glance. The first is this:

> sould to Thomas Sheuyntons sonne the belman & Tho dychers sonne 3 Course vestments & a course stremer to make players garments viij<sup>s</sup> Fol. 28<sup>v</sup>

The year is 1570, and the mystery plays have almost lived their date. One would give a great deal to know whether the son of "Thomas Sheuynton the belman" and "Tho dychers sonne" were outfitting professional actors. It would add a final touch of irony and grace to our sense of indebtedness to Mother Church if we knew that when evil days came upon her, the infant stage which she had done so much to foster benefited from the dispersal of her very garments.

For its own sake, even if it did not also suggest something of the temper of the last days of the religious drama in England, I add another item:

1573 payd 4 may 1573 for a great bible to serue the church xxvij<sup>s</sup>
for pharaphrases of Erasmus same tyme xij<sup>s</sup>

payd to Ed doby the glasior for mendinge of the glasse
wyndowes and defacinge of the Images in the same
accordinge to the quenes Iniunctions   x$^s$.

Fol. 30$^v$

In 1575 there is another payment to Ed Doby of 3$^s$ 4$^d$ for
"mendinge windows."[22] If the stained glass of the Middle Ages
could not outlast the Reformation, we could hardly expect the
teachings of the older Church, movingly set forth in liturgical
drama and mysteries and miracles, to survive.

There are no extant accounts of miracle plays or moralities
from Chester; and I shall leave the voluminous story of the
Chester mysteries to later lectures. It would be tempting to
spend some time with the Corpus Christi procession which
craftsmen entering their gilds were sworn to maintain; but as
it was not drama, but worship, I pass it by.

We must also pass by the Midsummer Show into whose gor-
geous *mélange* the mystery plays sent some of their most popular
figures: the Devil in his feathers, the Doctors and the "letall
[little] God," Balaam and the Ass, etc. But it will be proper to
point out that this show, an amazing cavalcade passing on Midsummer Day through the streets of Chester, contained giants, a
dragon, naked boys, morris dancers, and all manner of folk
elements not drawn from the mysteries, but derived from re-
motest antiquity.

We learn from Harley MS. 2125 that a play of St. George
was performed in Chester in 1429. St. George is, as we have
seen, one of the heroes of the mummers' plays, but we have also
seen that St. George plays were performed before Edward III
in 1348, at Coventry in 1474, and at Bassingbourne in 1511.
Tiddy tells us that "From the beginning of the fifteenth century
until as late as 1550 both the St. George and the Robin Hood
plays are mentioned frequently in the records of the civic com-
munities." He also suggests that after the Renaissance, "the St.

George plays became the property of the humbler classes exclusively."[23] This degeneration is perhaps not the only possibility; simple folk rituals could as well inspire more elaborate plays; and it is a fair guess that these plays of St. George and Robin Hood were offered by strolling players.

At any rate, folk games and revelry of all kinds flourished in Chester. In 1567 George Bellin tells us of a "lorde of misrule and other pastymes in the Cittye" to which he must have been an eye-witness.[24] But Merrie England was growing grim; and in 1556-7 the Mayor and Aldermen had solemnly enacted "that no maner of person or persons w[th]in this citty goe abrode a muminge in any place w[th]in the same Citty their faces beinge Couered or disgised & that no maner person or persons w[th]in this Citty suffer any person or persons to play at any vnlawfull games w[th]in his or their howse or howses, etc."[25]

From evidences of St. George and mumming plays, we may turn to an early example of the dramatic interlude in Chester. This is the play of *King Robert of Sicily* which was performed at the High Cross in 1529.[26]

The windows of the Pentice or City Hall looked directly out on the High Cross in the very heart of Chester. This play, therefore, must have had the official blessing of the Mayor and Aldermen. Chambers says that it "is doubtless the play on the same subject referred to in a fragmentary letter to some 'Lordshypp' among the State Papers as to be played on St. Peter's day at the cost of some of the companies. It was said to be 'not newe at thys time but hath bin before shewen, evyn as longe agoe as the reygne of his highnes most gratious father of blyssyd memorye, and yt was penned by a godly clerke.' "[27] I have not been able to pin down this letter. Chambers records a play on the same subject at Lincoln in 1453[28]; and if it were not for the fragmentary letter he speaks of, and its reference to "some of the companies," I should take it that the Chester performance was given by a travelling troupe. The subject is hardly one for a long play, but it is as suitable to a small interlude group as to the narrative pen of Longfellow.

If the liturgical plays and interludes can be illustrated by Chester records, so can the classical influence upon English drama. An eye-witness in 1564 tells us:

In this yeare the Sondaye next after Mydsomer daye there was a Tryvmpth devysed by Wyllyam Crofton gent. and one m<sup>r</sup> Man Scholemaister of the ffree Schole of the history of Aeneas and Quene Dido of Carthage, in w<sup>ch</sup> Trivmpthe vppon the Roode Eye was Two ffortes and a Shippe vpon the water with sundrye horssemen well Armed & appointed.

Additional MS. 29777

The City Treasurer's accounts for 1564[29] yield the following light upon this Triumph:

Itm paid m<sup>r</sup> mayre at midsomer for the trivmphe xxvj<sup>s</sup> viij<sup>d</sup>

. . . . . . .

. . . . . . .

Itm paid to houghe gillome for daunsinge at midsomer vij<sup>s</sup>

Itm paid Thomas yeaton for gonne poulder at the trivmphe by master mayres apoyntment xiij<sup>s</sup>

The large sum of xxvj<sup>s</sup> viij<sup>d</sup> no doubt went to the players. Gunpowder to emphasize the love of Dido and Aeneas may seem anachronistic; but that the subject reveals classical influence upon English drama there can be no doubt. Moreover, our scanty records show that the Triumph arose out of the collaboration of a Gentleman and a Schoolmaster.[30]

George Bellin tells us that in 1577 when the Mayor, Thomas Bellin, entertained the Earl of Derby and his son, Ferdinand Lord Strange, "the scollers of the frescole also playd a comedy before them at m<sup>r</sup> maiors howse." He tells us further that in 1588–9, "a play was playd at high crosse called the storey of kinge Ebrauk w<sup>th</sup> all his sonne but such rayne fell it was hindred much."[31] This play of King Ebrauk surely must have been a travelling play, for King Ebrauk or Ebrancus has no connection with Chester, but is a legendary hero of York. Cotton Julius MS. B. XII has an account of Henry VII's first progress to York and gives the verses that were spoken at the royal entry whose subject was Ebrancus.

I should like to close this lecture with a little glimpse into the lives of professional actors at the close of the sixteenth century. The following items come from the accounts of the Treasurer of Chester Cathedral:[32]

1583    Payd the xiij[th] of Maye unto Mr. Rogers whiche he gave to the Earle of Essex Players, when they woulde have played in Mr. Deanes house   ij[s].

1589    Itm to the Q Players, at the appoyntment of Mr. Deane & the Chapter   xx[s].

1590    Itm to the Queene Mats Players   xx[s] x[d]

1591    Bestowed upon the Earle of Essex his Musitianes   ij[s]

     . . . . . . . . . .

     . . . . . . . . . .

     To the Queenes players   xl[s].

The earlier entries concerning the Earl of Essex's players may also refer to his musicians, but the reluctance of the Dean and Chapter to hear them suggests that they were really actors. The Earls of Essex had maintained an acting troupe for more than a hundred years;[33] between 1581 and 1601 these actors visited many towns.[34] So far as I know, their visits to Chester have not been noticed. Nor have those of the Queen's players. It will seem remarkable that these should receive 20[s] and 40[s] for their efforts, while the Earl of Essex's players were fubbed off with 2[s], and probably not heard at all. The fact is that hostility to the stage was growing more and more virulent, so that in 1596 the Mayor and Aldermen ordered that "there shalbe neither play nor bearebeat" within the city, but reserved the privilege of hearing and rewarding the Queen's players with "twentie shillinges" and "any noble mans players sixe shillinges eighte pence and not aboue."[35]

Harley MS. 2173 contains copies of documents in the Mayor's chest made by Randle Holme in 1644. On fol. 81[r] there is a warrant of the year 1600 from Edward Lord Dudley to "francis Coffyn and Rich. bradshaw to trauell in the quality of playinge & to vse musicke in all Cittys Towenes & Corporations w[th]in her maiestyes dominions." This warrant was seized November 11, 1602, by Hugh Glaseour, Mayor of Chester. Richard Bradshaw and Francis Coffin and their company are not the last actors in the history of time to have been stranded, but it is hard to conceive of disaster more complete than that which fell upon them. They were not only refused permission to play in Chester; but, having lost their warrant, they were unable to play anywhere else. Their warrant "to trauell in the quality of playinge & to vse musicke" may dissolve the question whether the servants of the Earl of Essex were actors or musicians. They may have been both. Even at Shakespeare's Globe, music trims up the drama; and one can well imagine that travelling players, with catch-as-catch-can facilities, needed music even more.

The shades were closing down on Merrie England. In 1615 the Mayor and Aldermen of Chester, because of "the Comon Brute and Scandell w[ch] this Citie hath of late incurred and sustained by admittance of Stage Plaiers to Acte their obscene and vnlawfull Plaies or tragedies in the Comon Hall of this Citie," enacted that "from hensforth noe Stage Plaiers vpon anie pretence or color what soever shalbe admitted or licenced to set vp anie Stage in the said Comon Hall or to acte anie tragedie or Commedie or anie other Plaie by what name soever they shall terme it, in the said Hall or in anie other Place w[th]in this Citie or the Liberties thereof in the night time or after vj[e] of the

Clocke in the eveneinge."[36] The chances of being permitted to play before six in the evening, I leave to your imaginations.

At this point, then, I conclude the reading of the first lesson. No great addition has been made in it to previous knowledge of English drama in the Middle Ages—but I have been fighting Homeric battles in the Notes! Simply, the story has been summarized with sidelights from the records of Chester. Two minor suggestions have been made which may be worth the time given them: that various forms of rudimentary drama could co-exist, and that professional acting may be older than has been believed. In Chester within a single year one could have seen a liturgical play at Holy Trinity, an interlude at the High Cross, and multiple mystery plays at Whitsuntide. Within a single year one might have seen a Midsummer Show whose elements go back to pre-Christian times, a Corpus Christi procession, mumming plays at Christmas, and a Triumph with the classical story of Aeneas and Dido. And within two years of an attempted revival of the mediaeval mysteries in 1600, we have seen a troupe of professional actors stranded in Chester.

As for the professionals, Chambers believes that the last vestiges of the Roman theatre are to be found in travelling mimes and joculatori; but we know that various lords maintained players of interludes in the fifteenth century. These might well visit lords and nobles friendly to their masters; and, if so, they might also visit towns where their masters held respect and influence. To support this suggestion there is in an expense roll of St. Werburgh's Abbey the following entry,[37] apparently for 1525:

Et solut' diuersis nuntiis et histrionibus tam d'ni Regis quam aliorum magnat' pro diuersis vices eidem Abb'i accident'

13$^{\text{li}}$ 6$^{\text{s}}$ 8$^{\text{d}}$

The sum seems enormous to have been paid to visiting actors and messengers; but it certainly does imply that acting troupes were on the road early in the sixteenth century. My suggestion, therefore, that *King Robert of Sicily* was performed in 1529 by strolling players may seem reasonable.

In these records, also, we have seen the blight of Puritanism settling down upon Merrie England. The Midsummer Show, it is true, continued until 1678 when it was abolished by order of the Corporation,[38] and Chester did not, a century earlier, give up her mystery plays without a struggle; but, practically speaking, all the magnificent processional pageantry of the Middle Ages, all the mingled revelry and worship of religious drama, like the genuine but joyous reverence of Corpus Christi Day, melted into air, into thin air, and, in the third quarter of the sixteenth century, faded like a dream. It was then, although the Free School was active a generation earlier, that in Chester the Middle Ages died.

> Men are we, and must grieve when even the shade
> Of that which once was great is passed away.

HE REMAINING LECTURES of this series will be
devoted to the Chester Mystery Plays, their
history, and the way in which they were produced and performed. But, first of all, let us
look at the text of a typical mystery and learn
something of its character.

The play of Noah's Flood contains 372 lines. It can be read
in ten minutes, and presumably could be performed in less than
half an hour. The stage directions are in Latin. The first, being
translated, reads, "And first in some high place or in the clouds,
if it can be done, God speaks to Noah standing outside the Ark
with all his family." In forty lines God announces that He will
destroy the world, and commands Noah to build an Ark:

> 300 cubytes it shall be long
> And 50 of breadeth to mak it stronge,
> Of heighte 50. The mete thou fonge:
>     Thus measure it about.
>
> One wyndow worch through thy wytte.
> Onc cubyte of length and breadeth make it.
> Upon the side a dore shall sitt
>     For to come in and out.
>
> Eating places thou make also,
> Three roofed chambers, one or two;
> For with water I think to slowe
>     Man that I can make.
>
> Destroyed all the world shall be
> Save thou, thy wife, thy sonnes three—
> And all there wives also with thee
>     Shall saved be for thy sake.

29

Noah thanks God and turns to his family, requiring their help. All of them set to work eagerly, Sem with his axe, Ham with a hatchet, Japhet with a hammer to drive in wooden nails. Sem's wife finds a chopping block, Ham's wife gathers pitch to caulk the vessel, and Japhet's wife prepares food. Noah's wife is surprisingly willing to help, considering her later conduct, for she says:

> And we shall bring tymber to,
> For wee mon nothing els doe:
> Women be weake to underfoe
> Any great travayle.

No doubt she staggers in under a load that would collapse an ox! A stage direction now reads, "They make signs as if they were labouring with divers tools." Noah speaks of joining boards and raising a mast; and when the Ark is complete, he bids his wife enter.

She refuses, and Noah remarks to the audience in a Shakespearean aside that women are always crabbed. He appeals to her again on the ground that if she does not enter, the audience will think her the master of his household, adding under his breath, "And so thou art, by St. John!" We may note in passing the anachronism of having Noah swear by St. John—another truly Shakespearean touch!

At this point God speaks again, telling Noah to take into the Ark seven specimens of all clean animals and birds and two of all unclean ones, as well as food for all since the Flood will last "40 dayes and 40 nightes." We learn that the Ark has been a-building for 120 years, a time lapse that would have turned Shakespeare green with envy. The best he could do, even at the height of his career, was a meagre sixteen years or so in *The Winter's Tale* and *Pericles*.

The next stage direction reads: "Then Noah will enter the

Ark and his family will pass to him all animals depicted on cards, and recite their names; and after speaking his part each one of them, except Noah's wife, will enter the Ark; and the animals depicted must agree with the words spoken, and thus begins the first son":

> *Sem.* Syr, here are lyons, libardes in,
> Horses, mares, oxen, and sywne,
> Geates, calves, sheepe, and kine:
> Here sitten thou may see.

One manuscript says that the paintings of the animals are set up around the "boards" of the Ark, thus explaining the line, "Here sitten thou may see."

Now if this seems a crude way of presenting the story of Noah's Ark, let me ask how it could be done better even today. At Maskelyn's Theatre, London, a theatre devoted to magic and sleight of hand, with all the resources of modern, realistic stage apparatus, I saw an exactly similar show of Noah's Ark in 1930. Moreover, all the resources of Hollywood, unrestrained by a fixed stage and limitations of space, and capable of showing anything that an uninhibited camera can see or select, did little better with Noah's Ark when *Green Pastures* was produced.

Having got all living things aboard except his wife, Noah appeals to her again. She again refuses unless she can bring in her old cronies with her; and we have now a realistic little picture of mediaeval life as the Gossips say:

> The flood comes in full fleetinge fast;
> On every side it spredeth full fare.
> For feare of drowning I am agast:
> Good gossip, let us draw neare.
>
> And let us drinke or we depart,
> For often tymes we haue done so;
> For at a draughte thou drinkes a quarte,
> And so will I doe or I goe.

> Here is a pottell of malmsey good and strong.
> It will reioye both hart and tong.
> Though Noy thinke vs neuer so long,
> Yet wee will drinke alyke.

It need hardly be asserted that there are people, even among us, who would meet the end of the world in just this way. Truth to life is not peculiar to modern drama.

The sons carry in Noah's wife by main force while she struggles and lays about her with a will. Noah now "closes the window of the Ark, and after a little time they sing within, 'Saue me, O God.'" Afterwards, Noah opens the window and looks out, saying that forty days and nights have elapsed. He sends out a raven which does not come back. Then he sends out a dove; by a sleight another dove bearing a spray of olive is passed to him from inside, but he seems to pick it out of the air. All the characters now step out of the Ark and release the animals. God closes the play with sixty lines of instruction to Noah, and makes the covenant of the rainbow with him.

During three days in summer at various dates from the fourteenth to the sixteenth century one might have seen many such plays as this performed at various stations in the streets of Chester. Noah's Ark was appropriately produced by the craft gild of Waterleaders and Drawers of Dee; that is, by men who supplied the city with water in days when there was no city water system. The Tanners, who could provide the skin-tight, white-leather costumes necessary, originally produced the play of Adam and Eve; the Bakers had the Last Supper; and the cycle of plays covers the story of Man down to Christ's Ascension, the Sending of the Holy Ghost, Antichrist, and the Last Judgment. The plays of Chester are rather over-filled with didactic instruction; but most of them include such realistic or comic bits as those about Noah's wife and the Good Gossips.

During the sixteenth century a tradition grew up in Chester concerning the origin of the plays. It will be instructive to follow the growth of that tradition—and it may be equally instructive to see what modern scholars have made of it.

The first document in the tradition is William Newhall's Proclamation for the plays written in 1532. It is to be found in a "Book Containing Fragments of Assembly Orders" in Chester Town Hall; all of the materials in this book belong to the fifteenth and sixteenth centuries. The paper on which the Proclamation is recorded is rotted and eaten away at the edges. I shall present the document exactly as I saw it, except that contractions and abbreviations are silently expanded:

The proclamacion for the plaies newly made by Willm Newhall
      (               ) pentice the first yere of his entre

    fforasmoche as of old tyme not only for the augmentacion & incre(                  ) faith of o(    ) uyor ihu Crist & to exort the myndes of the common people (                 ) doctryne th(    )f but also for the commen welth & prosperitie · of this Citie a pla(           ) & diuerse storiez of the bible begynnyng with the creacion & fall of lucifer & (              ) iugement of the world to be declared & plaied in the witsonweke was devised & ma(         ) henry sometyme dissolued ffraunc(   ) monk of this monastery who obteyned & gate of Clement then beyng (             ) daies of par(    ) & of the busshop of Chestr at that tyme beyng xlv daiez. of pardon g(        ) thensforth to euery person resortyng in pecible maner with gode devocion to here & se the sai(       ) frome tyme to tyme asoft as they shalbe plaied within this Cittie ~~and that euery person (~~       ) ~~disturbying the same plaiez in eny maner wise to be accursed by thauctoritie of the sai(~~ ~~)~~ ~~pope clement(~~      ) ~~bulles vnto suche tyme as he or they be absolued therof~~ Whiche plaiez were de(    ) to

the honor of god by John Arneway then mair of this Citie of
Chestr & his brethern & holl cominalte therof to be brog(    )
forth declared & plaied at the Costes & chargez of the craftes men
& occupacions of (    ) said Citee whiche hitherunto haue frome
tyme to tyme vsed & performed the same accordi(    ) *Where-
fore* maister mair in the kyngez name straitly chargeth & com-
maundeth that euery person & (    ) of what astate degre
or condicion so euer he (  ·  ) they be resortyng to the said
plaiez do vse th(    ) pecable without makyng eny assault
affrey or other disturbans wherby the same (    ) shalbe disturbed & that no maner person or persons who so euer he
or they be do vse or we(    ) vnlawfull wepons within the
precynct of the said Citie duryng the tyme of the said p(    )
~~not only opon payn of cursyng by thauctoritie of the said Pope
element bulles but also~~ opon payn of enprisonment of their bodiez
& makyng fyne to the kyng at maister mairis pleasure and god
saue the kyng & m^r mair etc.

> per me W. Newhall factum tempore Willielmo Sneyde draper
> secundo tempore

Canon Rupert H. Morris some sixty years ago was able to
read more of this document than I have read, but he does not
reveal the true picture.[1] He does not indicate, for example, the
words inserted above the line. Further, he says that *in dorso* of
the Proclamation are the words: "The Proclamacion for the
fo....11 opon the rode ee made by the same William Newhall
the said first yere." Actually, these words appear on *the next
page.* Now one of the great events of the Chester year was the
football game on the Roodee on Shrove Tuesday; and that is
what these words *in dorso* actually refer to. The Plays were *not*
proclaimed on the Roodee. As in other cases, Newhall wrote
the heading and left the page blank, intending to fill in the
proclamation later.

Morris says further, "The proclamation is endorsed, 'The Proclamacion of the Plaie to be made on Satreday after the election, newly of Latin into Englishe translated, and made by the said William Newhall the yere aforesaid.' " There is no such endorsation, but several pages further on in the book there is the following heading over a blank page: "The Proclamacion of the Place to be (                    ) Satreday after the election newly also and (                    ) of laten into Englishe translated and made by the said William Newhall the yere aforsaid." It will have been noticed that Newhall spells the word plays, *plaies* and *plaiez*. Further, the proclamation he intended to fill in here was one for Saturday after the election. The Mayors of Chester were elected on October 9. Why should they announce in October the plays for the following summer? Whether the *play* Proclamation was originally in Latin, we do not know.

These errors of Morris have been taken over by E. K. Chambers[2] and others, and are now part of a modern legend concerning the Chester Mysteries.

The date of Newhall's Proclamation is 1532 when William Sneyde was Mayor for the second time and when Newhall became City Clerk.[3] The deletions will have been noticed. These remove from the Proclamation the reference to Pope Clement and the pain of cursing. Why did Newhall make these deletions? The answer will be obvious: in 1531 Henry VIII was acknowledged Supreme Head of the Church in England. Why, then, does any reference to Pope Clement remain? The answer is that none did—but I shall defer the proof for a moment.

There is a further curious detail. Why should Newhall write, "this monastery"? He is Clerk of the Pentice or Town Hall. It is as if standing on this platform in Hart House Theatre, I should speak of "this church." Now if the Plays were not proclaimed on the Roodee, where were they proclaimed? Obviously at the great public place in front of "this monastery"! Note also that Newhall has written above the line, "dissolued." But St. Werburgh's was suppressed only in 1539. Newhall must have worked on this Proclamation twice—in 1532 and in 1539 or 1540. But these facts have been obscured from modern scholars by Canon Morris's unfaithful transcript.

Let me point out also that according to this Proclamation the Plays were "devised and made by Sir Henry Frauncis," and they were "devised . . . by John Arneway." Does it not become clear that with the Disestablishment of the Church of Rome, the civic officials became anxious to remove from the Plays which ministered to the prosperity of their city any odour of Roman Catholicism? We may well surmise that only in 1532 or 1540 were the Plays removed from the jurisdiction of "this monastery dissolued" and taken over by the Town Hall. Such a possibility has never heretofore been suspected, but the large amount of pious didacticism in the Chester Mysteries is proof positive that they never did escape from the censorship of the Church of Rome before that Church itself was extinguished in England. To William Newhall, the Disestablishment meant that he had to write a new Proclamation for the Chester Mysteries, and he had to remove from them the taint of Rome and find a better authority. By 1532 the origin of the Plays was lost in antiquity. What could be more reasonable than to ascribe them to the man whom all the local antiquaries of the sixteenth century honoured as the first Mayor of Chester?[4] It would seem that Arneway first came into the picture at this point, and that the real initiator of the Chester Plays was Sir Henry Francis. He may actually have been the author of the first of them that appeared in English.

In another document, dated 1540,[5] we are able to see New-hall's finished work on his Proclamation. It is exactly, word for word, the same as the version we have been studying, except that *all* reference to Pope Clement and Henry Francis has disappeared. From it, the holes in the earlier document can be confidently filled in.

If the civic authorities of Chester had some difficulty in adapting their plays to the new régime in 1532 and 1540, they were to encounter still more trouble as the Reformation continued; and they responded in precisely the same way, trying to lend to the plays the prestige of unquestionable authority. The attack upon mystery plays became formidable all over England after the accession of Queen Elizabeth in 1558. A manuscript whose original seems to date from before 1575 makes the following statement:

The old and anchante whitson plaies, played in this Cittie of Chester, were first made, Englished and published by one Rondall Higden a monke of Chester Abbey; In the time of S^r John Arneway knight and mayor of Chester anno Dom. 1268, the last tyme they were played was anno Dom. 1571, m^r John Hankye then mayor of Chester.

Stowe MS. 811, fol. 19^v

For the first time Randall Higden is named as author of the plays. Just as Arneway was the first Mayor of Chester, Higden was Chester's greatest man of letters, the author of *Polychronicon* and other Latin works. It is quite possible that he knew no English.

The next statement in the growing tradition is to be found in the late Banns, or announcements for the Plays, which I have dated elsewhere 1575.[6] In these we have Sir John Arneway setting "out in playe The devise of one done Rondall, moonke of Chester Abbey." But the late Banns go a step further and turn Higden into a stalwart champion of Protestantism against Rome. "This moonke—not moonkelike" was "in Scriptures well seene"; and he "was nothing Afreayde with feare of hanginge, breninge or Cuttinge off heade, To sett out [the plays in English] that all maye disserne and see." We need not be surprised at this development. King John himself, of whom a contemporary chronicler had said, "Foul as it is, Hell itself is defiled by the fouler presence of John," became in the sixteenth century a pure and high-minded hero of the Reformation.

Sir John Arneway died in 1278,[7] Higden just eighty-six years later in 1364[8]—but how could the civic officials in 1575 be expected to know such trivial details? Even today, and among persons who have had some schooling, a sense of history is not common. What we are dealing with in Chester four hundred years ago is a habit of mind to which a century means nothing at all.

The manuscripts of the Plays themselves, all copied in the 1590's, muddy the waters considerably, for some of the scribes seem to have been in touch with pre-Newhall information. Thus Harley MS. 2013 has a small fly-leaf attached to one of the blank pages at the beginning, and on it is written in a hand earlier than that of the manuscript itself, the Proclamation made by Newhall, but retaining all the material which he had scored through. Now we have Pope Clement and Sir Henry Francis back in the tradition! But at the end of the Proclamation a later hand has added, "S^r Io Arnway maior 1327 & 1328 at which tyme these playes were written by Randall Higgenett a monk of Chester abby & played openly in the whitson weeke." As I have pointed out, Arneway could not have been Mayor in 1327 and 1328, for he died in 1278. I may add that in the early days the Plays were not performed in Whitsun week, but at Corpus Christi.

On the cover of Harley MS. 2124, another copy of the Plays, is written:

The Whitsun playes first made by one Don Randle Heggenet, o Monke of Chester Abbey, who was thrise at Rome before he could obtaine leaue of the Pope to haue them in the English tongue.

The Whitsun playes were play'd openly in pageants by the Cittizens of Chester in the Whitsun weeke.

Nicholas the fift Then was Pope in the year of our Lord 1447. Ano. 1628.

Sir Henry ffrauncis sometyme a Monke of the Monestery of Chester, obtained of Pope Clemens a thousand daies of pardon, and of the Bishop of Chester 40 dayes pardon, for euery person that resorted peaceably to see the same playes and that every person that disturbed the same to be accursed by the said Pope, vntill such tyme as they should be absolued thereof.

Surely this document represents nothing more than a frenzied attempt in 1628 to reconcile the irreconcilables brought into the story by William Newhall. Now it is not Henry Francis who was at Rome, but Randall Higden, although Francis secured pardon from Clement; and we have a new Pope in the picture, Nicholas V, dated 1447 so as to make him contemporary with Higden who died 83 years earlier. Perhaps this reconciler knew that Arneway died in 1278—and therefore omits him.

The Chester antiquaries of the sixteenth and seventeenth centuries all copy from each other. The only point of variation is the date they assign to the first Mayor and the first performance. The period of variation covers 71 years:

| | |
|---|---|
| 1268 | Stowe MS. 811; Additional MS. 11335. |
| 1269 | Liber N, Tabley House; Harley 2125(2). |
| 1320–1 | Harley MS. 1046. |
| 1327 | Harley MS. 2125 (1). |
| 1328 | Harley MS. 1944. |
| 1329 | Additional MS. 29779. |
| 1339 | Harley MS. 1948. |

Still other dates are given to the mayoralty of Arneway in other manuscripts. In each of these manuscripts the date is said to be that of the first performance of the Plays, the author is said to be Higden, and the Mayor is said to be Arneway. Although they follow their fancy in dating, these antiquaries are curiously dependent upon each other in wording. For example, every one of these manuscripts lists twenty-five plays, and every one of them states that there were twenty-four.

Just as William Newhall is responsible for the whole tangled skein I have been presenting, so the whole modern legend about the Chester Plays derives from the monumental *Mediaeval Stage* of E. K. Chambers. Inadequately informed by Morris of the true nature of Newhall's Proclamation, Chambers grapples manfully with the problem. And it was no schoolboy problem he had to solve. In a word, how could the Plays have been "devised" by Sir John Arneway, "devised and made" by Sir Henry Francis, and "first made, Englished and published" by Randall Higden? What was the date of their origination, and which of the fourteen Popes named Clement was involved? That is, if the Pope was not Nicholas V.

Chambers finds a Mayor of Chester in 1327–9 named Richard Herneis. Sir John Arneway and Richard Herneis are names in his opinion so similar that they might easily be confused. Moreover, "About 1328," he says in his *Mediaeval Stage*, "is just the sort of date to which one would look for the formation of a craftcycle."[9] And, as Randall Higden took Holy Orders at St. Werburgh's in 1299, he could have written the Plays thirty years later in the mayoralty of Richard Herneis.[10] (In his recent *English Literature at the Close of the Middle Ages*, however, Chambers admits that Higden's authorship of the Plays "is not very plausible."[11] But he still feels that 1327–9 is a likely date for the origin of the cycle.) The role of Sir Henry Francis he dismisses as merely that of a person who gained pardon for the Plays' spectators. "The Pope Clement concerned," says Chambers, "is probably Clement VI (1342–52), but might be the Antipope Clement VII (1378–94)."[12]

There are, however, some troublesome facts. First, England did not subscribe to the authority of the Antipope: we may

eliminate that Clement. Second, Sir Henry Francis was Abbot
of St. Werburgh's, and signed two agreements with the rectors
of Taxall and Gawsworth, one in 1377 and one in 1382.[13] Since
Clement VI died in 1352, it is hardly likely that Sir Henry
Francis who flourished from twenty-five to thirty years later,
dealt with him. But is it not curious that the Pope with whom
Henry VIII quarrelled in the years prior to 1532 when Newhall
re-wrote the Proclamation, was another Clement VII? He died in
1534. Sir Henry Francis did have to do with a Pope, however,
for he was made a Papal Chaplain in 1389 by Urban VI.[14]

I have tried to show that there was a strong ulterior motive
for deleting the references to pardon by Pope Clement from the
official Proclamation in 1532; and I have tried to show that
there were powerful ulterior motives for bringing in the names
of Arneway and Higden; but if we now eliminate from our
belief all that incompatible nonsense about Higden and Arneway, we shall find ourselves up against the solid weight of almost
unanimous modern scholarship on this subject which all stems
from Chambers.[15] Nevertheless, we must look at the Chester
Plays in the light of the times in which they were performed.
When we do so, we are left with the simple statement in the
Proclamation which William Newhall revised in 1532, that the
Plays were "devised and made by Sir Henry Francis." Nothing
could be more explicit. Moreover, no ulterior motive can be
found for Newhall's statement about a man whom Chester had
forgotten.

If we accept this statement as truth, we at once eliminate a
part of the supposed great antiquity of the Chester Plays. They
cannot have been devised in or before 1328 by a man who flourished sixty years later. But the moment we accept the possibility
that the Plays were initiated by Sir Henry Francis, we find that
they come into being at the very time when we have our earliest
references to mystery plays elsewhere, for the earliest firm refer-

ences to English mystery plays are to those of Beverley in 1377,[16] York and London in 1378,[17] and Coventry in 1392.[18] It may be that Sir Henry Francis was honoured by Pope Urban VI for his work in religious drama. If so, the date of the origination of the Chester cycle would be about 1385. Yet it would be a shame to take away from Chester that pride of priority in which she has gloried for four centuries. Let us date her Plays 1375 and let her precede Beverley by a full two years!

With this date, everything falls into place and becomes intelligible. At that very period, for example, there was a great surge of new interest in the English language which had become official in the law courts in 1362. There had been, it is true, a few preliminary attempts, mostly in romances, to restore English to England; and in 1349 John Cornwall had departed from all precedent and had his children construe their Latin in English. Before 1370 Chaucer had made his momentous decision to write in English. It is quite possible that, at any rate in England, the mystery or craft plays were translated out of Latin at the same moment when they were brought outside the church. There are no plays surviving in England, which, linguistically or otherwise, show any traces of greater antiquity than the last quarter of the fourteenth century;[19] and there are no firm references to mysteries at any earlier date.

We may believe, with Chambers, that the Corpus Christi festival first suggested processional performance of the plays, but his statement that "The English miracle play [read *mystery*] reaches its full development with the formation of the great processional cycles almost immediately after the establishment of the Corpus Christi festival in 1311"[20] is certainly incorrect by more than a hundred years. Nobody has ever found a firm reference to craft plays in England before 1377; and at least in Chester, the "full development" did not arrive until the reign of Henry VIII, almost two hundred years after 1311.[21]

It will seem to many in this audience that I have been trying
to shake the foundations of a fabric of knowledge of the mystery
plays of England carefully built up by generations of excellent
scholars. Well, one good turn deserves another: let me hurl another brick.

Modern scholars assume that the plays were secularized the
moment they became cyclic.[22] Actually, in England they remained under the jurisdiction of the Church as long as the
Church of Rome itself endured. Where did the opposition to
the plays come from? It came from the Church of England, the
new Church. Why should the new Church be opposed to
*secular* plays? There could be no reason at all. But the new
Church was bitterly hostile to anything that smelt of Rome, and
the mystery plays were nothing more or less than most active
and impressive propaganda for Roman doctrine.

Further, why is it that so few manuscripts of the plays survive
in England when we know that these plays were produced in a
hundred towns? The answer is that the new Church destroyed
them, as the works of the Devil and Rome should be destroyed!
The story of the Paternoster play of York is illuminating. Archbishop Grindal in 1572 asked to see the manuscript. It was
given to him; and it has never been located since, even though
the civic officials tried for some years to get it back.[23] Rossiter,
therefore, is singularly wide of the mark when, following Chambers, he says, "The documents of the first secular plays would
naturally tend to vanish in the world's fires and ruinations, since
they were not in the safe keeping of long-lasting organizations
such as the abbeys and the guilds."[24] They were never secular,
the mystery plays, but religious; and they *were* in the keeping of
the abbeys and gilds; but to the gildsmen they lost all value, and
the abbeys became Protestant.

No doubt the reason why scholars speak of the plays as having
been early secularized, or divorced from the Church, is that they

contain comic passages. But things that may seem shocking or irreverent to us were not necessarily so to our ancestors; and anyone who knows anything about the Boy Bishop and the Feast of Fools, or the Feast of the Ass, which some voices even then condemned, will not question the hospitality of the ancient Church to materials which we would consider sacrilegious. There is absolutely nothing in any of the surviving mystery plays of England that would not have been decorous and seemly compared with the licentious doings of the Feast of the Ass before the High Altar itself, especially in France.

Once we entertain the possibility that the plays remained until 1531 under the jurisdiction of the Church of Rome, we shall find all sorts of corroborative evidence. For example, there was not a single town in England where the first and sometimes the only performance did not take place at the abbey, cathedral, or church before the pageants were wheeled on to other stations. Why? Because the Church kept its grip and its censorship.[25] Again, whenever we find a statement hostile to the plays, they are not called civic plays or craft plays, but Popish. And then, why is it that the same subjects are treated in the same way, except for minor differences, all over England? So great is the homogeneity of material that in the past scholars have tried to discern the features of a single "parent cycle." Is it likely that civic authorities or craft gilds would lend manuscripts and materials to each other? About as likely as that modern business firms would lend trade secrets! But Mother Church was concerned only with spreading the faith. You could have heard the same trope in any of a thousand churches from Dublin to Constantinople in the earlier Middle Ages, just as you could have heard the same Mass, on the same day. The homogeneity of material in the mystery plays is due to the same universal or catholic reason.

In Chester, at any rate, the mystery plays were Church plays until 1531. One swallow may not make a summer, but if the mediaeval Church is involved, one swallow is as good as a whole migration. What the Church did in Chester, the Church did everywhere: the mystery plays were never secularized at all. When the Church of Rome vanished, and a virulent Protestantism replaced it, the plays staggered on for fifty years because of their tremendous popularity and their value to business; but in the end they had to go—and leave behind, as I shall try to show in the next lecture, a violently hostile annalist in the son of Archdeacon Robert Rogers of Chester.

Let me now attempt a brief history of the Chester cycle. The first outdoor performance in English was devised about 1375 by Sir Henry Francis. It is probable that a single long play was produced, for the appearance of the Doctor or Interpreter in play after play of the late series suggests an original single work. This single ancestor again suggests stationary performance.[26] At what time this play was broken up, and when it became processional, we do not know; but we do know that individual gilds had their own plays as early as 1422. In that year a quarrel arose between the Ironmongers and the Carpenters as to which of them were entitled to the assistance of the Bowyers, Fletchers, Stringers, Coopers, and Turners in the production of their play of Corpus Christi. The jury decided on oath that the Bowyers, Fletchers, etc. had their own play of the Flagellation of Christ, and the Ironmongers the following play of the Crucifixion. The Carpenters also had a play of their own. This is not named, but the Wrights, presumably the same gild, later had the Salutation and Nativity.[27]

Chambers says that the civic plays of Chester were always performed at Whitsun,[28] but the document which records this quarrel speaks of Corpus Christi plays, thus proving that the plays did become processional by falling in with the Corpus

Christi festival. The cycle was not performed every year, however, while the Corpus Christi procession was annual. The earliest reference I have found to *Whitsun* plays in Chester is in an agreement made in 1521 between the Smiths and the Founders and Pewterers whereby these gilds were "fully condescendet & agreid to berre & drawe to whitsun playe & Corpus Christi light."[29]

After 1422, the next record of the Plays is an item in the City Treasurer's accounts for 1429–30. He received from the Fishmongers a rental of $4^d$ for a piece of ground on which to store their pageant wagon, next to the door of the Friars Minors. This piece of ground and this rental appear in the accounts from 1429–30 to 1441–2. Thereafter the Fishmongers disappear, and the Drapers seem to have taken over that piece of ground. This land the Drapers continued to rent for one hundred years; and they paid for it the same rental in 1539–40 that they paid in 1461 and 1467.[30] The Fishmongers must have made other arrangements for their pageant wagon, for they continued to produce until the very end their play of Pentecost.

The same record of rentals shows that the Mercers had a play in 1437–8, the Shearmen (Cissorum) in 1439–40, the Saddlers, who rented a place called Truants' Hole, in 1467–8. The Saddlers rented the same piece of ground in 1539–40.

The story of the Shearmen is rather involved. They were organized as a gild as early as 1423–4 when they may also have had a play.[31] In 1430 it was agreed in Portmote that each member of the gild of the Weavers, Walkers, Chaloners, and Shearmen must pay toward the upkeep "& expenses del lumeir de nostre dame sainte marie & de corpus xpi & al Iwe de Corpus xpi & a lun & lautre de eux a toutz & a chescun . . . la some a quele il est assesse par lez ditz seneschalles."[32] We must note that the Weavers and the Shearmen who later had separate gilds with separate plays, are here members of a single gild. The

Tailors also complicate the picture. Although they are not mentioned in this agreement, they must have belonged to this gild; but they have a separate play later, and the language of the early Banns (1467)[33] seems to suggest that their play had been newly brought in.

The Saddlers may also have acquired their play shortly before 1467–8 when they rented Truants' Hole. Their charter of 1471–2,[34] granted to endure for forty years, seems designed specifically to organize them so that they may produce a play. In this charter, the Plays are still spoken of as "pagine luminis et ludi corporis christi."

The Bakers had a charter dated January 12, 2 Edward IV (1462).[35] Members of the gild must "be redy to pay for the Costes & expences of the play and light of Corpus Christi as oft tymes as it shall be asseset by the same stuards for the tyme being."

By 1467–8, then, we know that eight gilds in Chester were producing plays. I shall list them and the plays they held in the late series:

Drapers. Play II. The Creation; Adam and Eve

Wrights. Play VI. The Salutation and Nativity

Mercers. Play IX. The Gifts of the Magi

Bakers. Play XV. The Last Supper and Betrayal

Bowyers, Fletchers, etc. Ironmongers }Play XVI. The Flagellation and Crucifixion

Saddlers. Play XIX. Christ on the Road to Emmaus

Fishmongers. Play XXI. Pentecost

Shearmen. Play XXII. Prophets before Antichrist

We cannot say that in 1467 there were no other plays than these in the cycle. The early Banns of that date provide for not eight, but eighteen plays; but some of these had been introduced

after the Banns were first written, so that they disrupted or dis-
located the stanzas of the text.[36] In the Mayor's Book for 1475,
nineteen gilds are listed, apparently play-producing gilds. A
document of 1500[37] definitely, and not merely apparently, lists
play-producing gilds, and names twenty-four of them, including
one group that is not a craft gild, "ye wyfus of ye town." From
other evidence we know that the Wives produced the Assumption of Our Lady. The early Banns of 1540 announce twenty-
six pageants, and the late Banns of 1575 show the cycle reduced
again to twenty-four. The Wives and the Assumption had dropped out, and so had the Tapsters and Hostlers who had previ-
ously produced a play of the Harrowing of Hell.

Between 1467 and 1540, then, the cycle grew from eighteen
to twenty-six plays. No doubt a similar growth preceded 1467.
But the exact story is excessively complicated. As the generations
passed, a flourishing gild might decay and find itself no longer
able to bear the expense of a play; or a new gild might spring
up and take on such an obligation. Further, individual groups
of craftsmen associated themselves variously from time to time,
and all these changes in the organizations producing the plays
brought about changes, makeshifts, and adaptations in the plays
themselves. Some pageants, like the Assumption of Our Lady,
might be presented or not with no great injury to the cycle; but
when an essential play like the Crucifixion could no longer be
brought forth by its sponsors, something had to be done; and,
as an example in point, when the bow and arrow yielded the day
to firearms, and the Bowyers, Fletchers, and Stringers could no
longer provide the Flagellation, this play was combined with
the Crucifixion of the Ironmongers, and the two gilds under-
took a new single play. It is for this reason, incidentally, that all
the antiquaries of Chester *say* that there were twenty-four plays,
and then *list* twenty-five. This amalgamation of the Flagellation
and the Crucifixion was the very last of the many adaptations

to changed circumstances that the cycle experienced. In a word, then, the history of the Chester cycle, and no doubt of every other cycle, is a story of continual change, makeshift, and adaptation, withal a story of growth, so that the cycle saw its golden days in the period of Henry VII and Henry VIII when some stability came to England after the long misery of the Wars of the Roses.

Individual plays from the cycle seem to have been produced for special occasions, but our only evidence to this effect comes from local antiquaries of the late sixteenth and seventeenth centuries. Although they repeat each other word for word, they become hopelessly confused about dates. Thus we learn that the Assumption of Our Lady was played before Prince Arthur on the following dates:

    1496   Additional MS. 29780; Stowe MS. 811(fol. 48$^r$)
    1497   Harley MS. 2125
    1498   Additional MSS. 11335, 29777, 29779; Liber N, Tabley
               House; Stowe MS. 811(fol. 20$^r$)
    1499   Harley MS. 2133

If we believe these manuscripts, we must surmise that the Assumption of Our Lady had something to do with the feeble health of this boy prince who died in 1502 at the age of sixteen. But the truth is that Arthur never saw the Assumption at all. What he saw was the Purification—and he saw that in 1499. My reason for saying so is that his blacksmith was a Chester man; and Book I of the Smiths' Company records that "Thomas Dyan Smith to Prince Arthur being at the castle of Chester in the fourteenth year of the Reign of Henry the Seventh, his Father then being King of England, and at the same time Prince arthur gave unto the said Dyan a Crown of Silver Gilt, a hammer with Horse Shoe and Pincers the Arms of Smiths to them and their Successors for euer." If any further evidence is needed to clinch the matter, then I can produce the unimpeachable authority of Harley MS. 2057 which says that not the Assumption, but the Purification was played before Arthur—but I regret to say that it has slipped on the date, giving 1498 when it should be 1499. Perhaps I should add that the Blacksmiths who dealt with white hot steel and purifying flames were the appropriate gild to bring forth the pageant of the Purification.

Without going into a similar mix-up regarding dates, it can be asserted that the actual date when the Assumption was separately played was not in the 90's, but in 1488 before the Lord Strange;[38] and the reason why it was singly performed may have been that it was then a new play produced by the Worshipful Wives of the city.

Harley MS. 2125 tells us that the Assumption was played separately again in 1515, and the Shepherds Play along with it. It records also that in 1578, after the last performance of the full cycle, the Shepherds Play was again performed in the Mayor's house before Ferdinand Lord Strange.

The story of the last days of the mystery plays in England has been told by H. C. Gardiner, S.J. in a volume entitled *Mysteries' End*.[39] He correctly ascribes the demise of the plays not to the financial difficulties of the gilds, but to the hostility of the new Church. Chester evidences bear out this thesis, but there is a record of one Andrew Tailer, a dyer, in Chester, who went to gaol rather than pay his share of the pageant expenses of his gild in 1575.[40] If Andrew Tailer went to such extremes, no doubt many others grumbled. But it was the Privy Council itself, under the Queen the highest power in the realm, which gave the Chester Plays their *coup de grâce*.

There is one curious incident, however, just before the Privy Council took action, which I am at a loss to interpret. Randall Trever got possession of the official Register of the plays some time before 1568. In that year before the Mayor and Council he swore "upon the holy evangelist of God" that he had returned

it, but he could not name the person to whom he had given it.[41]
The Register has never been seen since. You will recall that the
last person known to have handled the Paternoster play of York
was Archbishop Grindal. The stories are similar. A few details
can be advanced about Trever, but nothing significant. He was
a physician who witnessed the will of Rob[t] Backe of Manchester
in 1556; he inherited money and land by the will of Christopher
Butler in 1557;[42] and in an inventory of the goods of Randle
Leche in 1580 there is a list of "Debts Counted desprat," of
which one is, "docter treuor 21[s]."[43] But he seems to have no dis-
coverable connection with either the Church or the Privy Council. If I have, nevertheless, suggested some smell of skulduggery
about the good Archbishop of York and the good physician of
Chester, I have suggested no more than I intended. Plays were
produced in a hundred towns; hundreds of manuscripts of them
existed in the mid-sixteenth century; the loss of all but the most
pitiful handful is due to a far more burning hostility than that
of "the world's fires and ruinations."

The following statements are typical of those of local antiquaries concerning the last years of the plays, and as antiquarian
interest first announces itself at this time we may accept these
statements as true:

1572    This yeare the playes were plaid, but an inhibition came
        from the Archbushop of Yorke, to stay them, but came
        not in time.

1575    the plaies likewise this yeare plaied at Midsomer, and then
        but some of them leauing others vnplayed which the
        Maior was ioyned not to proceed there withall.

                                                    Harley MS. 2057

1575    this yeare the said s[r] John Sauage caused ye popish plaies
        of Chester to bee playd ye Sunday Munday Tuesday and
        Wensday after Midsummer day in contempt of and Inhi-
        bition and ye primates letters from yorke and from ye

Earle of Huntington, for which cause hee was serued by
a purseuant from yorke, ye same day yt ye new Maior
was elected, as they came out of ye common hall, notwithstanding the said S^r John Sauage tooke his way towards
London, but how his matter sped is not knowne Also M^r
hanky was serued by the same Purseuant for ye like contempt when hee was Maior, diuers others of ye Citizens
and players were troubled for ye same matter.

Harley MS. 1046

Sir John Savage found himself in real trouble. He seems to
have been accused of wilfully and single-handedly ordering the
Plays, and a letter from him in London to the Council begs them
to send him a certificate that the action of ordering the Plays
was not his only but that of the whole Council. This certificate
was duly sent. With this letter and this certificate,[44] the history
of the mystery plays in Chester comes to an end, although there
seems to have been an attempt to revive them in 1600.[45] From
that time onwards, the Plays lay dormant and neglected until
the present Poet Laureate drew from them inspiration and material for new religious plays staged at Canterbury Cathedral,
and until in 1953 they became at their proper home, old St.
Werburgh's itself, part of the celebrations which marked the
Coronation of our new Gloriana, Elizabeth II.

If in this lecture I have truncated the period during which the
Chester and other cycles of mystery plays are said to have flourished, I trust I have not destroyed any element of their human
interest, but, perhaps, drawn them into sharper focus for modern
appreciation. In them, just as in the fabric of the great cathedrals of an earlier age, we see the whole community at work in
one great co-operative enterprise dedicated to brisk business and
the glory of God. I mean nothing irreverent by this remark: the
cathedral of the Middle Ages was spacious and hospitable enough to include all the elements of human life; and in stained
glass and carvings and statuary all the means of human liveli-

hood, the sower and his seed, the smith and his anvil, the fisher-
man and his nets, and all the arts and crafts of life found their
due place within the House of God. And not only men and their
sports and occupations: the beasts of the field and the birds of
the air were not forgotten, nor were the creatures which peopled
the mediaeval imagination—dragons and unicorns, angels and
saints, and a host of most engaging or terrifying imps and devils.
The mystery plays brought religion out of the cloister and the
cathedral to blossom in spectacle and verisimilitude along the
streets. They ministered to the same love of the picturesque as
the Pasadena Tournament of Roses, the fantastic floats of a
football game, or the Calgary Stampede, that nostalgia for days
that never were when Indians lived in full regalia and cowboys
were larger than human, heroes and not hirelings.

But if, equally with the modern Trade Fair, the plays had a
part in the business life of the town, they nevertheless remained
under the strict jurisdiction and censorship of the Church as
long as the Church of Rome endured in Chester and—I believe
—in England. Thereafter, a sneaping wind tarnished their finery;
and, without ecclesiastical support, indeed with ecclesiastical
hostility, no matter how urgently business interests tried to keep
them alive, they were bound to decay. Their primal function,
after all, was religious, and no amount of cutting and patching
could take away from them the taint of Roman worship.[46] Living images of the Roman doctrine, they, like the stained glass
windows of Holy Trinity, had to vanish. John Hanky, Sir John
Savage, and the Common Council of Chester to the contrary
notwithstanding, Carthage had to be destroyed.

# A DAY'S LABOUR

HE EARLIEST ATTEMPT to describe the production and staging of the Chester Mysteries is to be found in the *Breviarye* of Chester history, ascribed to Archdeacon Robert Rogers, but actually compiled by his son, David Rogers, in the seventeenth century, at least one generation after the last performance of the Plays—and probably two. The earliest copies of this *Breviarye* are Harley MSS. 1944 and 1948. These vary slightly in form and wording, but they are the onlie begetters of a great many, if not all, of the later accounts of the Chester Plays. Associated with the great name of Robert Rogers, the *Breviarye* has been granted the authority of an eye-witness account, although there is hardly an accurate statement about the Plays in it, and although the author was by no means in sympathy with his subject.

Archdeacon Rogers died in 1595 or earlier.[1] Morris therefore dates the *Breviarye* 1590.[2] But Harley 1944 contains the Banns of the Plays as they were revised for a projected revival in 1600. These are signed D. R., apparently the initials of David Rogers. Harley 1948 says on fol. 18ʳ that the materials "were collected by the Reverend mʳ Robert Rogers . . . and written by his sonne David"; but it has an account of the St. George's Day Race on the Roodee, starting, "In anno Dom. 1609, Mr. William Lester, etc.," and ending, "This was the first beginninge of St. George's race, etc." It seems unlikely that Archdeacon Rogers, who was certainly dead by 1595, collected this item after 1609. Further, this statement surely cannot have been written in the very year when the St. George's Race was first

54

organized. Indeed, there is a later reference to a change made in the Race in 1623. Nevertheless, Chambers dates both Harley MS. 1944 and Harley 1948, 1609.[3] Doing so, he sails very near the wind.

Even if the *Breviarye* had been written in 1609, that date is thirty-four years later than the last performance of the Chester Mysteries; and a boy who was sixteen in 1575 would be fifty in 1609, sixty-four in 1623. It could fairly be questioned whether David Rogers ever saw the Plays at all.

Nevertheless, for what it is worth, here is the account of the Chester Plays from Harley MS. 1944, fol. 21ᵛ:

Now of the playes of Chester called the whitson playes when they weare played & what occupationes bringe forthe at theire charges the playes & pagiantes.

Heare note that these playes of Chester called the whitson playes weare the woorke of one Rondall a moncke of the abbaye of St. Warburge in Chester, who redused the whole history of the byble into Englishe storyes in metter, in the englishe tounge, and then the firste mayor of Chester, namely Sir Iohn Arneway knighte he caused the same to be played, the manner of which playes was thus: They weare deuided into 24 pagiantes or partes, and euery Company brought forthe their pagiente which was the cariage or place which they played in: And yarlye before these were played there was a man fitted for the purpose [fol. 22ʳ] which did ride as I take it vpon St. Georges daye throughe the Citie and there published the tyme and the matter of the playes in breefe which was called the readinge of the banes. They weare played vpon monday, tuseday and wenseday in witson weeke. And they first beganne at the Abbaye gates & when the firste pagiente was played at the Abbaye gates then it was wheeled from thence to the pentice at the high

*These playes are now abollished*

*yeurely*

*April 23*

crosse before the Mayor, and before that was donne
the seconde came, and the firste wente into the
watergate streete & from thence vnto the Bridge-
streete, and soe all one after an other tell all the
pagientes weare played appoynted for the firste
the descrip-    daye, and so likewise for the seconde & the thirde
tion of the     day: these pagiantes or cariage was a highe place
pagintes the    made like ahowse with ij rowmes beinge open on *Room*
played in:      the tope the lower rowme they apparrelled & dressed
them selues, and in the higher rowme they played,
and they stoode vpon 6 wheeles And when they had
done with one cariage in one place they wheeled
the same from one streete to an other. first from
the Abbaye gate to the pentise then to the watergate streete, then to the bridge streete throughe the
lanes & so to the estgate streete. And thus they came
from one streete to an other keapeinge a direct
order in euery streete, for before the first cariage
was gone the seconde came, and so the thirde, and
so orderly till the laste was donne all in order without any stayeinge in any place for worde beinge
broughte how euery place was neere done they
came and made no place to tarye tell the last was
played.

At this point in Harley MS. 1944, the Banns follow. These do
not appear in Harley MS. 1948. In the latter manuscript also
the carriages have four wheels rather than six. The attitude of
David Rogers may be seen in the following statement which
appears next after the Banns in Harley MS. 1944:

And thus much of the Banes or Breife of the whitson playes in
Chester for if I shoulde heare resite the whole storye of the whitson playes it woulde be too tediouse for to resite in this breauarye
as alsoe they beinge nothinge proffitable to any vse, excepte it be
to shewe the Ignorance of oure forefatheres. and to make vs theire
ofspringe vnexcusable before God that haue the true and synceare
worde of the gospell, of our lord & sauioure Iesus Christe, if we
apprehende not the same in oure life & practise to the eternall

glorie of our god and the saluation & comforte of oure owne soles:
Heare followeth all the Companyes as they weare played vpon
theire seuerall dayes, which was Monday: Tuesday: & wenseday
in the whitson weeke And how manye pagiantes weare played vpon
euery day at the Charge of euery Companye.[4]

At this point Rogers lists twenty-five plays, although he has
just told us there were twenty-four. It is difficult to believe that
so hostile a witness ever actually saw the Plays. One thing he
certainly did not see was the riding of the Banns, for the Banns
were not *read* by one person as he says, but *ridden*: every company sent out its representatives for the occasion in the costumes
in which they played on the great day itself. No doubt it is
from this *Breviarye* that Randle Holme gets the idea that the
City Crier rode the Banns, for in the accounts of the Smiths
in Harley MS. 2054 (see below p. 76), he has tacked on "the
citty Crier ridd" to the item, "for ridinge the banes xiij[d]." If
every one of the twenty-four or twenty-five gilds in Chester
paid the Crier 13[d] for riding the Banns, that gentleman, as I
shall presently explain, must have had one of the best grafts
in history. David Rogers, also, has given us in his account other
statements which I have shown in previous lectures to be un-
true. We would do better to base our ideas of the production
of the Chester Plays upon other evidence.[5]

Let us start with the Pageant Houses. These were simply
large sheds in which the wagons or carriages which served as
stages for the mystery plays were stored. Unfortunately, our
ancestors did not know that we might be curious about such
things, and the records which they kept for their own purposes
are not very illuminating.

The earliest records about the pageant houses are to be found
in Harley MS. 2158 in which Randle Holme copied as well
as he could a number of rolls of the Murengers and Treasurers
of Chester. He seems to have been most careful in copying, but

the rolls had suffered seriously before he got hold of them. He explains the fragmentary nature of his copy by frequent remarks such as, "Roll 9. A bundle of Rentalls both broke & obscure but by the hand & names should be in Ed. 4 tyme & part of H 7"; "Roll 11. This Roule much decayd but abstracted what may be legable"; "Roll 34. a broken peece of a Treasurers Roll temp. Jo Southworth maior 18 E 4." The rolls from which he copied ran from 1435–6 to 1482–3. I have already drawn upon them for information regarding the possessors of plays; and need only repeat here that the Drapers, the Fishmongers, the Mercers, the Saddlers, the Shearmen, and the Tailors rented from the City places where they maintained pageant houses.[6] The rental paid by the Fishmongers was 4[d] a year. The Mercers paid 6[d].

The next record in time is an agreement made in 1531 between the Stewards of the Vintners and those of the Dyers on one hand and the Stewards of the Goldsmiths and Masons on the other that the Goldsmiths and Masons may have free use of the carriage of the Vintners and the Dyers providing they pay a yearly rental and sustain "the thrid parte of all & euery reparacon" and "the thrid part of all the rents due or to be due for the house wher [the] said Cariage now standeth or hereafter shall stand."[7] Unfortunately, this record is fragmentary, and time has carried away the very thing we should like most to learn: i.e., the amount of money involved. But the language, "the thrid parte," etc. suggests that the carriage was already shared in 1531 between the Vintners and the Dyers who had separate plays; and that it was now to be shared by a third gild, the Goldsmiths and Masons. By means of this document, we can nail down one inaccuracy in David Rogers' account of the plays. He says, "euery Company brought forthe their pagiente which was the cariage or place which they played in." Actually, there were fewer carriages than plays; and the Vintners, the Dyers, and the Goldsmiths shared a single stage. How could they do so?

As the cycle comes to us, the Vintners had the play of the Magi, no. VIII, performed toward the close of the first day. The Goldsmiths had Play X of the Slaughter of the Innocents, the first performance of the second day. And the Dyers had Antichrist, no. XXIII, played toward the end of the third day. One carriage could readily be adapted to all their needs.

The next document is a record of City rents in the time of Henry Gee, Mayor, 1539–40. It is to be found in handwriting of that date within Harley MS. 2150; and it lists rents received by the City from the Shearmen, the Smiths, the Tailors, the Saddlers, the Drapers, and the Mercers. The Shearmen, Smiths, Tailors, and Saddlers each pay $4^d$; the Mercers $6^d$; and the *Rent* Drapers $8^d$. Some of these gilds occupy the same places as they had occupied a century earlier. Here is the record itself:

*The Northgate strete*

The occupacon of Shermen for A place to sett theire cariage    iiij$^d$.

The occupacion of the Smythes for A place to sett theire cariage adionyng to the Shermen vnder the walles negh vnto a Towre called the Dilles towre    iiij$^d$.

. . . . . . . . . . . .

. . . . . . . . . . . .

. . . . . . . . . . . .

*Lovelane*

. . . . . . . . . . .

. . . . . . . . . . .

. . . . . . . . . . .

The occupacion of the tailleours for A cariage house by yere    iiij$^d$.

. . . . . . . . . . .

. . . . . . . . . . .

. . . . . . . . . . .

The occupacion of the Sadlers for a place called truantes hole by yere    iiij$^d$.

. . . . . . . . . . . .
. . . . . . . . . . . .
. . . . . . . . . . . .

*Gray ffrere Lane*

The occupacion of the drapers for A certeyn place to byld on whiche thei putt theire carriage in nigh to the yate of the ffreres mynors be yere   viij$^d$.

The occupacion of the mercers for a certeyn place to byld A house on in the whiche thei putt theire cariage   vj$^d$.

We may be puzzled by the statement that the Drapers and the Mercers are to build; both have been paying the same rentals for a hundred years. Perhaps it was necessary to rebuild.[8]

Whatever the number of the Plays—and I have tried to show that there were twenty-six in 1540[9]—we know that during the fifteenth century the Drapers, Mercers, Saddlers, Shearmen, and Tailors had pageant wagons, as they still had in 1540. We know that the Fishmongers also had had a wagon in 1435, but it is not recorded in 1540; and we know that in 1540 the Smiths had a wagon. We know, further, that nine years earlier, in 1531, the Vintners, Dyers, and Goldsmiths agreed to share a carriage; and the rental paid by those gilds which paid ground rent to the City was between 4$^d$ and 8$^d$ a year.

The next carriage of which record exists is that of the Coopers. In 1572, the Coopers "reseuyd of the paynters and of the skynners for the caryge x$^s$ viij$^d$." In 1574, they "received of the stuardes of the paynters for our cariadge, v$^s$ iiij$^d$" and "of the stuardes of the hatmakers & skynners v$^s$ iiij$^d$."[10] This also was a convenient arrangement, for the Painters had the Play of the Shepherds on the first day; the Coopers had the Trial and Flagellation of Christ, performed on the second day; and the Skinners had the Resurrection of the third day. It would seem unlikely that there ever were as many carriages as plays; half as many would be a fair guess.

Five shillings and fourpence is an enormous rental to pay for a carriage. We have seen that the pageant houses which sheltered the wagons rented at from fourpence to eightpence a year. If we think of a modern garage as renting for $90 a year— as it does in Edmonton—and equate that sum with sixpence, then 5/4 would be worth on the same scale eleven times as much, or roughly $1000. For a thousand dollars we could build a quite elaborate "float" for a modern parade. These carriages were not built for that sum; they rented for it for one day's use.

Obviously, so large a figure for one day's rental cannot be correct. Another record will enlighten us. In 1574, Richard Dutton, Mayor, leased the Tailors' carriage house to Robert Hill.[11] The Tailors had paid a rental of 4$^d$, but Hill was to pay 2/6. The rentals paid by the craft gilds, therefore, must have been nominal; and if the ratio of 4 to 30 represents the ratio between the nominal and the actual value, we could simply divide the end-figure of the calculations above ($1000) by seven. In that event, we should find a day's rental of the Coopers' carriage worth about $135. Even this figure is startling.

The value of money, it need hardly be said, is difficult to work out. We all know that at the time when the King James Bible was translated, a penny was a fair wage for a day's work. That is what the workers in the Vineyard received. In Harley MS. 2093, fol. 33, rates of pay are listed for all the trades in Chester for an earlier year, 1592–3, when, because of near-famine, all prices had gone up. The highest pay for a day's work, "with meat and drink," is 4$^d$ for master carpenters. Mill-wrights receive 3$^d$; smiths, wheelwrights, and plowwrights, 2$^d$; rough masons and bricklayers, 2½$^d$; plasterers, sawyers, lime-

makers, brick-men, tilers, tile-makers, 2$^d$; the remainder, 1$^d$.[12]
If we equate the penny with the eight or nine dollars a day that
rough labour now receives in Edmonton, then a carriage renting
at 5/4 brought in something over $500 for one day's use. It
must have been a most elaborate and expensive vehicle. Let
us say that this attempt at equating values is completely wild;
but even if we divided $500 by five, we must still be dealing
with a carriage that is a great deal better than makeshift.
Indeed, the very fact that it was stored from year to year
suggests a vehicle worth storing.

Robert Hill's lease might have been more useful to us than
it actually is. The Tailors' carriage house is described in it as
being 5 royal virgates long, and 3½ virgates wide. The trouble
is that we don't know the length of a virgate! According to the
*Oxford Dictionary*, it was equal in the eighteenth century to a
rod or pole, i.e., 16½ feet; but a carriage house more than 80
feet long and 55 feet wide is surely unlikely. Before the standard-
ization of weights and measures, these varied greatly all over
England. The virgate may have been only a yard. Randle Holme
so translates it in the seventeenth century.[13] But if his yard was
the same as our yard, a building 15 feet long by 10½ feet wide
would seem too small to accommodate a carriage which could
rent at certainly more than $100 for one day's use.

Our difficulties in interpreting records regarding the carriage
houses are not solved by records of the carriages themselves. We
have accounts of the expenses of the Coopers' gild for the production of their play in 1572 and 1574.[14] This gild did not rent
a carriage house, but took their wagon apart each year and
stored it in John Joanson's cellar. In putting it together, getting
it and their gear painted, using it, with 2/4 paid to the "putters"
on the day of the plays, and breaking it down again for storage,
they spent in 1572, 27/10. That is, they spent 334$^d$, more than
the equivalent of a man's wage at rough labour for a full year.

In modern terms, the day's use of their own carriage came to more than $2500.

In case our ideas of the size and equipment of the mediaeval stage should become too inflated, however, it should be pointed out that seven men could place the stage and haul it around the town. Only, those seven men received 2/4 for their day's work— that is to say, 4[d] each, which, as we have seen, was the highest wage any craftsman could receive for a day's labour during the inflation of 1593. The money paid to the "putters" suggests that they had horses, but there is no actual mention of horses in the Chester records.[15]

The accounts of the Smiths exist for the years 1554–78.[16] This company made a special assessment of its members in the years when they produced their play; and the normal individual contribution of the thirty-one gild members was 2/4. Perhaps I should point out again that gild members were *not* the "simple craftsmen" continually spoken of by modern scholars as the producers of mystery plays. They were *employers*. Can you believe that an ordinary craftsman would be able to give a full month's wages for the production of plays? The records show that while the gildsmen of the Smiths paid 2/4 each, the whole body of journeymen altogether gave 5[s], perhaps a penny or halfpenny each.

In 1561 the Smiths built a new carriage, and in 1562 they paid the Weavers 4[s] presumably as rental for a place in which it had been stored. This item continues to appear in their annual accounts. The total cost of building and preparing and using the carriage in 1561 is 38/4¼, and we cannot be sure that some further costs may not be disguised in the accounts, or omitted. Even so, 38/4 was a goodly sum of money in days when it could buy a man's labour for a full year and a half. Or, said otherwise, a decent man could support his wife and family for a year and a half on the sum of money which the Smiths paid for building a carriage in 1561. If they had parts of an older vehicle which could be used again, even 38/4 would not represent the full value of the new one.

Of course the cost and comfort of living, or the living standard, has risen greatly in the Western world since the sixteenth century. It is hardly correct to say that a peasant in the Far East today gets the same reward for his day's rough labour as a workman in Canada. Nevertheless, making all allowances, 38/4 was a large sum of money in the sixteenth century. The carriage of the Smiths, however, must have been smaller or less cumbersome than that of the Coopers, for they paid only 18$^d$ to the putters of it, while the Coopers paid 28$^d$.

The point I am leading up to so tediously is this: that the mystery plays must have had stages that were sizable, with ample floor space for quite elaborate spectacles. We may turn now to the plays involved—those of the Smiths, Skinners, Coopers, and Painters—and ask what these plays demanded of the stage in the way of properties, space, and equipment.

Play VII, the Painters' Play of the Shepherds, seems to require a mound or hill. When the Third Shepherd comes in, he says to the First:

> Hankin, hold up thy hand and haue me
> That I were on height there by thee.

Of course, these lines might mean that the Third Shepherd comes on to the open space before the carriage, and asks for help to get on to the stage itself. But in l. 217, there is a further reference to "this hill." It is a sizable hill since the Three Shepherds and the Boy Trowe are able to move about on it, and even to engage in wrestling matches. At l. 310, there is a stage direction (in Latin), "Then they will sit down, or walk about, and the star will appear." Where does this star appear? We have seen that it was possible to rig up a moving star within the church at an earlier date; a less satisfactory mechanism would hardly be acceptable at a later time when the plays had developed further. At l. 368, a stage direction reads, "Then the Angel will sing 'Gloria in excelsis.' " In one manuscript the music is provided for this hymn. Where is the Angel while singing? He is not seen. At l. 474 we are told, "And the Angel will appear." Later he disappears. How are these appearances and disappearances managed? The Angel could hardly clump on to the stage with the same sort of entrance that other characters have. At l. 470, the Shepherds travel toward Bethlehem; and at l. 492 the First Shepherd exclaims:

> Here I see Mary
> And Ihesu Christ fast by,
> Lapped in hay.

There is no other reference to the stable or to the ox and ass, but these would be obligatory—and, in fact, the Painters' accounts for 1568 have the following item: "payd to tho beryg for payntyng of our ox & asse & our pyg in the common hall iiijᵈ." Whether the ox, ass, and pig were fabricated animals or paintings on a backdrop, it is evident that the Painters did try to represent a stable.[17]

The Shepherds Play, then, requires a mound at one side of the stage, a stable at the other, a moving star, and an appearing and disappearing angel. No doubt there is a "discovery" of the stable with Mary, Joseph, and the Babe; that is to say, at the appropriate moment curtains are drawn disclosing them. The Painters' accounts for 1561 have a payment of 3ᵈ "for 3 Curten cowerds." Sir E. K. Chambers says that the scenery of the mysteries "must have been rather sketchy, to allow of a view from all sides."[18] But I do not know how a stable can be viewed from all sides, especially if it has a backdrop and discovery.

The Coopers had the same carriage the next day for the Flagellation of Christ. At the beginning of the play Christ is led before Annas and Caiaphas, the high priests. One would expect them to appear high, placed on raised seats of some sort. At l. 72, a direction reads, "Then the Jews place Jesus in the cathedra." In classical Latin, *cathedra* is only a chair; but we are not dealing with classical Latin; in mediaeval Latin, according to DuCange, a *cathedra* was a church. Later in the play, Jesus is despoiled of His garments and bound to a column. Further, the Coopers in 1574 paid Richard Doby 2ᵈ, for what service we are not told. Richard Doby was a glasier.[19] I suggest that the *cathedra* of the Flagellation play is represented by a window, perhaps even a stained-glass one, at the mid-rear of the stage.

In addition to the *sedes* for Annas and Caiaphas, this play requires *sedes* for Pilate and Herod; but it is noticeable that the stage direction says that *two* of the Jews lead Jesus to Herod, while the whole crowd appears before Annas and Caiaphas and before Pilate. It would seem that the pageant wagon has now been pushed to the limits of its space; if we are to have *sedes* for three separate officials, and a representation of a church with columns and altar window, something has to be scamped—and Herod *is* scamped.

The general lay-out of the stage, however, is similar to that needed by the Painters who used the same carriage with a hill on one side, the Holy Stable on the other, and an open space between. Now in 1572, the Coopers paid "for the payntyng of our gere iijˢ viijᵈ." This is an enormous amount of money when we realize that it would secure the services of an unskilled workman for forty-four days, and of a workman of the highest skill for eleven days. What was there about a pageant wagon that required so much painting? The account for 1574 has a similar item: "Ite paied for the payntynge the playars clothes, ijˢ viijᵈ." But surely the players' costumes could not have been painted, for these were largely ecclesiastical garments. I take it that what was really painted were *cloths*: curtains, backdrops, and scenery;

and that the Painters trimmed up for the Coopers a simulated church with columns in the foreground, to one of which Christ was bound.

The Skinners also used the Coopers' carriage for the Resurrection. This play needs a *sedes* for Pilate, and it needs a Tomb large enough for a man to enter; indeed, large enough for two angels to be seen within, for there is a stage direction, "Then two angels, after Christ has risen, will seat themselves in the Sepulchre, of whom one will sit at the head and the other at the foot." Further, the three Mary's enter the Tomb and look around. This Tomb, with a different exterior appearance, could be the same structure that serves for a mount or hill in the Shepherds Play. Just how Christ *rises* in this play must be left, for the moment, to speculation. The stage direction reads: "Then two angels will sing, 'Christ arising from the dead, etc.,' and Christ will then rise, and, the song having been finished, will speak as follows." But how Christ leaves the stage after His speech, we are not told. It would hardly seem likely that He merely walks off.

The Smiths had a different carriage; and we do not know whether they shared it with any other gild. Their play combines two incidents that seem difficult because of the time element: the first is that of Simeon receiving the infant Jesus; the second is that of the boy Jesus among the Doctors. Both parts need a representation of the inside of a temple, and there is, again, an appearing and disappearing angel. At the beginning, Simeon reads in the prophecies, "Behold a Virgin shall conceive and give birth to a child." In doubt and bewilderment, he erases the word Virgin and writes in, "A good woman." He places the book on the altar, and the angel appears and writes the original word Virgin in bright red letters. This "business" is repeated; and in the end the angel appears to Simeon and tells him that he will not taste death before seeing the Redeemer. Mary then enters with the infant Jesus, and at the conclusion of this episode Simeon sings, "Nunc dimittis."

Returning now to David Rogers, we may ask some obvious questions. He says, "these pagiantes or cariage was a highe place made like ahowse with ij rowmes beinge open on the tope the lower rowme they apparrelled & dressed them selues, and in the higher rowme they played." Unless the wagons were built like pyramids, they could not have borne the weight on top required for a tomb above a dressing room—and for appearances and disappearances there simply must be some sort of machinery *above* the stage. Our ancestors did not have at their service actual angels who came fluttering down from Heaven when required. But, so long as there is a roof over the stage, and a bit of thin wire is available, anybody can contrive a satisfactory appearance and disappearance of heavenly creatures. A white costume against a white gauzy background will also very efficiently create an illusion of appearance and disappearance— but even this trick is impossible on a stage open to the heavens. The Coventry records have many references to a "wynd" and windlass, obviously for hoisting angels.[20] But the angels cannot be hoisted and left in the air: they must be hoisted into a disappearance, i.e., into a roof.

Further, what are the acoustics of the open air? A normal speaking voice can be heard at perhaps thirty feet; surely children, women, and angels in the plays did not shriek and bawl their parts so as to be heard by thousands of spectators. Even our crude ancestors would hardly require the Virgin Mary to bark and bellow like a sergeant major on parade. When the Mayor and Aldermen sat in the Pentice to hear the plays, they must have been at least fifty feet from the stage. And though the crowds at the Roodee stood on the hillside up which voices might rise, the actors would still need a sounding board. That sounding board a roofed wagon supplied.

A roof was also necessary to protect the rich vestments borrowed from the Church. The sunniest spot in all England can hardly boast more than fifty days of uninterrupted sunshine in the year; and one light shower would cause expensive damage.

Finally, corroboration of the roofed stage may be found in the expenses of the Coventry Smiths who in 1480 "paid to a carpenter for the pagent rowf vj$^d$."[21] Similarly, a Norwich pageant described in 1565 had "a square topp to sett over y$^e$ sayde Howse."[22]

We should remember that religious plays began within the church before the High Altar, that is to say, on a roofed stage. When they moved outside the church, it was simply a matter of placing the chancel, choir and altar and all, first on a platform at the great west door, and later on wheels. How, otherwise, did James Burbage come to think of placing a roof over the stage in the first theatre built in England? He roofed his stage because the stage had always been roofed, even when it was only a wagon blocking the entrance to an inn; and the stage had always been roofed because a sounding board was necessary, to say nothing of machinery and apparatus for ascensions and descents.

Indeed, when Shakespeare in *Cymbeline* has Jove sweeping down from the heavens upon the back of an eagle, hurling thunderbolts as he descends, he is using stage machinery which has been in existence for hundreds of years; and when Sir James Barrie in *Peter Pan* shows the children in flight about their bedroom, he also lies under direct debt to the makers of mystery plays—those crude ancestors of ours—half a thousand years ago.[23]

Let us question the stage requirements of some other plays.

In the Ascension of Our Lord, Play XX, after Jesus appears
to the Disciples in the upper room and is made known to them
in breaking the bread, the stage direction tells us, "Then He will
lead the disciples into Bethany, and when He arrives at that
place, Jesus, standing in the place where He will ascend, says
. . . ." Of course! What else are we to expect? There has to be
a *place where He will ascend*, a place where the machinery is
ready to draw Him up—and while He speaks, the necessary
fittings are unobtrusively arranged. The next stage directions
are also interesting: "Then Jesus will ascend, and while ascending He will sing as follows"; and, "Having finished the song,
Jesus will stand in the midst as if above the clouds." Hereupon
the First Angel will demand:

> Who is this that commeth within
> The blisse of heauen that neuer shall blyn?
> Blody out of the world of synne
> And harrowëd hell hath he.

After further speeches, we are told, "Then He will ascend, and
the angels will sing the following hymn while He ascends." Then
the angels descend, singing, "Men of Galilee, what do you
gaze upon in the heavens?" Then they in turn ascend once
more. How can all this ascending and descending be done in
"an open place on top of a wagon"? It can be done on a roofed
stage, and clouds can be painted on a backdrop or arranged
with gauzy hangings—indeed, at Chelmsford in 1562, fifty
fathoms of linen were bought to make clouds[24]—and it can be
a scene of great beauty and devout reverence, impressive in
holiness, if only we get rid of the naïve notion that our ancestors
were childish and crude.

A play which must have had similar machinery is the
Assumption of Our Lady which was eliminated from the cycle,
for obvious reasons, early in the sixteenth century. This play

is said to have been performed *solus* at the High Cross in 1488; and, seeing that there were no women actors on Shakespeare's stage, it is interesting to note that the Assumption was produced, and no doubt performed, by the Worshipful Wives of the City. But in other plays also women took their parts as naturally as men.

In the Creation when Cain and Abel prepare sacrifices, that of Cain is left untouched on the altar, for he has tried to cheat God. He says:

> Hit were pittye, by my penne,
> This eared corne for to bren!
> Therefore the diuill hang me than,
>     And Thou of this get ought!

> This earles corne grew nye thc waye.
> Of this offer I will to daye;
> For cleane corne, by my faye,
>     Of me getts Thou noughte!

Then he addresses his sacrifice to the Lord:

> Loe, God, here may Thou see
> Such corne as grew to me;
> Part of it I bring to thee
>     Anon, withouten let.

> I hope Thou wilt quite me this
> And sende me more of worldlie blisse;
> Els, forsoth, Thou doest amisse,
>     And Thou be in my debte.

Abel sacrifices in better spirit, and the stage direction tells us, "Then a flame of fire will come upon the sacrifice of Abell." How this flame of fire was managed, I do not know; but the trick was an ancient one. In the days of Alexander the Great, one "Kratisthenes could make fire burn spontaneously."[25] And the flame that descends upon the sacrifice of Abel is nothing more or less than evidence of the continuity of mime, juggler, and magician down through the Dark and Middle Ages.

We have heard often enough of the Hell-mouth belching fire and smoke in the mystery plays. There is no Hell-mouth in the Chester Judgment Play; but the Demons make a grisly job of carrying off the wicked to Hell. Before passing on, I may stop just a moment with the grave of Antichrist. The speakers refer to laying the body of Antichrist under the earth and gravel. After a time he rises to prove his godly powers. The stage directions refer to his *tumulus*, whereas the Tomb of Christ is called *Sepulchrum*. In other words, there has to be a pit or trap in the floor of the stage—the grave of Ophelia has a somewhat dishonourable ancestry.

In would be easy enough to devote an entire lecture to stage apparatus alone, but let us fry some other fish. Here are the expenses of the Coopers for their play in 1572:

The v nouembr elyzabeth by the grase of god quene of englande frans and yyerland defender of the fathe etc. the xiiij yere of hyr rene then beynge mayre John hanke

reseuyd of the paynters and of the skynners for the caryge    x$^s$ viij$^d$.

reseuyd of robbart carran that he was be hende    v$^s$.

.          lede done of expenses

In primis the herryng of the playeres and leuerynge of percells to the holle ys    1$^s$ [These are what we would call try-outs to select actors, and preparation of "sides" or actors' parts.]

Item spend at the forst reherse & the delyueryng of oure gerre to payntter    x$^d$

Item coste the brekynge of the caryge the bernggyn yt up to y$^e$ stuerdes doure    xviij$^d$

Item too selles to the caryge the pryse    ij$^s$ viij$^d$

more payde to John croulay for the makyng of y$^e$ caryge and nayles    iiij$^s$

Item for y$^e$ carynge y$^e$ welles to the water and frome & y$^e$ berygh of y$^e$ caryge   vij$^d$

more spende whan ye payntars come to garne y$^e$ bereghe[26] and at the seconde reherse in the stuardes lenekers   ix$^d$

Itm for ieren & byndyng of a welle & one stable one neue welle and the dresyng of our howlde welle the wyche comes to v$^s$ j$^d$

more spende in greseynge of the caryghe welles and grese to yt the ladar & the settyng vp of yt one the welles   xiij$^d$
[The ladder was perhaps a means of access to the stage for the actors.]

more for frettes & for axeltre penes   viij$^d$

Item spende at the brengeng vp of yt to y$^e$ menster gatte for cordes & penes to sette vp the howlynge of the caryghe   ij$^s$

more spend at dener on the company & one players and at nyght whan the vndressed them and all the daye   vij$^s$ viij$^d$

payde for the carynge of pylates clothes   vj$^d$

payd to wyllyam Rogerson for a cope & a tenekell   vj$^d$

payde to wyllyam twilloke by y$^e$ consant of y$^e$ company   vij$^d$

payde to vij men putters of the caryghe   ij$^s$ viij$^d$

payde to hugh gyllam   iij$^s$ vij$^d$

payde to Thomas marler   ij$^s$ iij$^d$

payde to John stynson   ij$^s$ iij$^d$

payde to rychard kalle   xvj$^d$

payde to hugh sparke for ryedyng of the Ryegenall   ij$^s$

Item payde to John proulay for the brekyng of y$^e$ caryghe   vij$^d$

Item payde to John Joanson for laynge the caryghe in his seller xviij$^d$

more spend at y$^e$ takyng done of yt & y$^e$ laynge in of yt   vij$^d$

Item payde for the payntyng of oure gere   iij$^s$ viij$^d$

The some ys in all y$^t$ the playes lyes in xlix$^s$ x$^d$

The accounts of the same company for the year 1574 help us to interpret these:

20 Nov. 1574

Item receaved of the stuardes of the paynters for our cariadge v$^s$ viij$^d$

Item received of the stuardes of the hatmakers & skynners v$^s$ iiij$^d$

Item spent in our aldermans at the rydinge of the banes xij$^d$

Item spend in horsbred vj$^d$

Item paied for wryttinge the parcell vj$^d$ [i.e., players' parts]

Item paied for ij paare of gloves vj$^d$

Item spend apon Thomas marler to get him to pleay ij$^d$

Item geven to william Rycharson ij$^d$

Item spent at the receavinge custome iij$^d$
   [This company farmed the customs at the Eastgate.]

Item spent at the fyrste rehearse vj$^d$

Item spend at the secunde rehearse xij$^d$

Item spend at the thred rehearse xij$^d$

Item paied for a peare of whelles iiij$^s$

Item geven to the presonars when we rode the banes ij$^d$
   [Such gifts on special days are regular in the Chester accounts.]

Item paied for nealis to the cariadge xij$^d$

Ite spend at the dressinge the cariadge x$^d$

Ite paied for the payntynge the playars clothes ij$^s$ viij$^d$

Ite spend on margery gybbon to get our regynale ij$^d$
   [Harley MS. 2173, fol. 96$^r$, has a record of a fine levied on "margery gibbons for keepinge an vnruly howse ij$^s$" in 1576. The Company probably kept their records in a trunk at her tavern.]

Ite paied vnto Robart slye for helpinge at the cariadge v$^d$

Ite spend at our generall rehearse  ij$^s$ x$^d$

Ite for a borde to the cariadge  iiij$^d$

Item for nealis to neale the hingis  ij$^d$

Item spent at the Bringinge vp the cariadge  viij$^d$

Item spent on Rychard Doby  ij$^d$

Item spent on Edwarde porter & for ij ropes  viij$^d$

Item nealis pynnis and cordes & drynke at the bowinge of our cariadge vj$^d$

Ite at the fyrste dresinge the cariadge for cordes  ij$^d$

Item for newe housinge to our cariadge  vj$^d$

Item for thre clapes of Iren to the cariadge  xvj$^d$

Item for the mendinge of arrats vysar  iij$^d$

Item spent at the Bowinge of the players  ij$^d$

Item paied for drynke to the players  ij$^s$

Item spent at the vnbowninge of the players in drynke & bred  xij$^d$

Item paied vnto pylat and to him that caried arrats clothes & for there gloves  vij$^s$

Item paied vnto the turmenters  iiij$^s$ vj$^d$

Item paied vnto annas  xxij$^d$

Item paied the pullers of our cariadge  ij$^s$ viij$^d$

Item paied the wright for settinge vp our cariadge & taking yt done and asonder  ij$^s$ x$^d$

Item spend at the takinge downe of our cariadge on som of our compeny  xij$^d$

Item spend at the receavinge of our mony for the cariadge of the paynters  iiij$^d$

Item entringe a accion agaynste Jhon ashewode and for the arestment of him  viij$^d$

Item more spent when we went to paye the players  vj$^d$

Item paied houghe sparke for redinge the regynall  ij$^s$

Item spent on medsomer even apon the company　v$^s$ iiij$^d$

Item spent at the Bowinge of our boye to ryde Before us　viij$^d$

Item geven to the presoners on medsomer even　vj$^d$

Item paied for the rent of our mettinge house　ij$^s$

Item paied & spent at the makinge vp of our bouke　xij$^d$

Another expense account may be added. It is that of the Smiths who produced the Purification. The account is for 1554.[27]

*Whitson plays*

for ridinge the banes　xiij$^d$　　the citty Crier ridd [This comment is added by Randle Holme.]

spent at potyng oute off Carriges at Rich barkers　4$^d$

we gaue at geting oute of the carriage　ij$^d$

we gaue for an axeyll tre to Rich belfounder　vj$^{d28}$

for an other axeyll tre to Ric Hankey　iiij$^d$

payd for dressing of the Carriage　x$^d$

for Ropes nelles pyns sope & thrid　x$^d$

for wheate　ij$^s$ ij$^d$　　for malt　iij$^s$ 4$^d$　　for flesh　ij$^s$ x$^d$

for flesh at the breckfast & bacon　ij$^s$ 8$^d$

for 6 chekens　x$^d$　　for 2 cheeses　xvj$^d$

Item we gaue for gelldinge of Gods fase　xij$^d$

Item we gaue botord beere to the players　4$^d$　　for bred in north-gate street　ij$^d$

we drank in the watergate street　vj$^d$　　at jo a leys　x$^d$　　at Ric. Anderton founderer　xij$^d$　　at m$^r$ dauison tauarne　xiij$^d$

to the mynstrells in mane [money]　ij$^s$

we gaue to the porters of the Caryegs　ij$^s$　　for gloues　xiij$^d$

we gaue to the docters　iij$^s$ 4$^d$

[i.e., to the High Priests in the Temple—or to the actors who played these parts. Since payments to Simeon follow, we learn

that the two parts of this play were combined as early as
1554.]

we gaue to Joseph   viij$^d$

we gaue to letall God  xij$^d$     we gaue to mary  x$^d$     to
Damane [Dame Anne]  x$^d$

we gaue to the Angells  vj$^d$     to ould Semond [Simeon]  iij$^s$ 4$^d$

we gaue to barnes & the syngers  iij$^s$ 4$^d$
  [Sir Randall Barnes was a minor canon and singing master at
  Chester Cathedral.]

for more wheate  18$^d$     malte  ij$^s$ ij$^d$     flesh  3$^s$ 4$^d$
  a chese  ix$^d$

to Randle Crane in mane [money]  ij$^s$
  [Morris, p. 350, says that Randall Crane was a minstrel.]

spent at mrs dauison tauarne  ij$^s$ j$^d$     for the charges of the
  Regenall  xij$^d$

to the skaynares  iij$^s$

for making of the Copes  v$^s$     for dressinge of the stands & jand-
  dases  xij$^d$

for gelding of the fane & for Cariiages of the lightes  xij$^d$
  [*Fane* could be either temple or flag.]

                                        In all iij$^{li}$ 4$^s$ 7$^d$

If we take money at our former valuation, and say that a
penny would buy a day of unskilled labour in the sixteenth century, and $8 or $9 will buy the same today, then we must reckon
that in 1554 the Smiths paid about $6000 to produce a play of
336 lines consisting of two short scenes which could certainly be
performed in twenty minutes. Of course there were several performances—indeed, four: at the Abbey, at the High Cross, before the Castle, and on the Roodee. The Painters in 1568 spent
not £3/4/7, but £4/2/6. It is true a good part of the money
went into food, drink, and rejoicing; nevertheless the plays were
expensive.

Now in a day when a penny was a fair—or an accepted—
wage for a day's labour, what about Old Simeon who received
forty times that amount, 3/4? Was he an unskilled actor?[29] It
is not the general nature of business men to pay for services
more than the services are worth; and the inescapable fact is
that the Smiths paid Simeon 3/4 at the same time that they paid
the workmen in their shops a penny or less for a day's work. Fees
on the same scale may be found in other expense accounts, not
only at Chester but everywhere. Surely there can be no escape
from the conclusion that the professional actor had a part in
these plays; and if so, he must go much further back into history than we have assumed. Old Simeon had to get 3/4 for his
day's work because his working days were few; and it may well
be that the "letall God" who took the part of the child Christ
before the Doctors, was his apprentice. Those actors who received tenpence or less may have been talented local folk.

That professional actors were abroad in the land long before
the sixteenth century, we may be perfectly sure—but I need not
again labour that point. Only, when we find on the title-pages of
morality plays statements like "foure men may well and easelye
playe thys Interlude," or "foure may easely play this playe"
(*Impacyente Pouerte*, 1560; *Welth and Helth, c.* 1525), we can
be sure there is a reason for such a general recommendation.

Further, when the gilds paid actors forty times what they
paid the journeymen in their shops, would they be content with
stuttering, inadequate, inaudible performance? We have seen
that they held as many as four rehearsals, of plays that average
four hundred lines. No doubt, part of the large fee granted the
actor is due to the time spent in preparation; but the four rehearsals also indicate anxiety that the plays be acceptable to
God and man.

The records show concern also that the actors be properly
clothed and made up for their parts. The clothes of Pilate and

Herod seem to have been rather special, for both of them had pages to hold up their trains ("Payde for the carynge of pylates clothes vj$^d$"; "Paied vnto pylat and to him that caried arrats clothes & for there gloves vij$^s$"). The face of the "letall God" was gilded for the day; and Joseph is represented with "beard like a buske of breeres With a pownd of heare about his mouth and more." The accounts of the Painters for 1575 show that they spent 6$^d$ "for the hayare of the ij bardes and trowes cape." In the same year they spent 3$^d$ for "ij gat skynes for trow shous" (Trow's shoes; Trow is a comic character in the Painters' Play), and paid "peter of mosten for makynge of trouwes shoues & hys paynes xij$^d$." Herod's visor, which cost 3$^d$ to mend, must have been an improvement upon nature. But perhaps the most interesting costume is that of Satan in the Creation play. He says:

> A manner of an Adder is in this place,
> That wynges like a byrd she hase,
> Feete as an Adder, a maydens face.

He proposes to adopt this semblance, and later says, "My adders coat I will put on." Shakespeare's Caliban has no wings. He is, rather, a manner of a fish. But the habitat, *par excellence*, of fabulous creatures is the Middle Ages. We may confidently say that Ariel in flight is a manner of an angel, and Caliban is not the son of Sycorax alone.

We look back sometimes with a sort of nostalgia to the Middle Ages when the artistic talent of every individual in every department of life could find expression. There were no assembly lines, then, to destroy the soul of a man; the individual was not an expendable cog in a vast machine; and we treasure today surviving pieces of their handiwork which must have been commonplace to them. If the gilds seized in the mystery plays the opportunity to advertise the handiwork by which they earned their bread, they can hardly be blamed. There is even, in the late Banns of Chester, a suggestion that the Bakers distributed samples to the crowds! They are told to "cast god loaves Abroade with A Cheerfull harte." Nor should we be shocked at the general jollification in which they indulged during the supreme event of their year. The amounts they spent on food and drink seem incredible—but so they are at a modern convention of the Rotarians or Shriners. Of one thing we can be certain: the mystery plays were extremely expensive to produce, and they required the zealous effort of the whole community. If, with all that labour and all that cost, they failed to attract the artistic genius that flowered so abundantly in the Middle Ages, one ought to be astonished. But the question of their intrinsic and artistic value is one which I shall leave to another lecture.

# A GREAT RECKONING

T IS CUSTOMARY to look upon the mystery plays of the late Middle Ages as the crude and childish productions of a childish and crude people. Bernhard Ten Brink long ago said, "Only a few details made any aesthetic effect—such as character, situation, scenes; the whole was rarely or never dramatic."[1] Katherine Lee Bates admits that "A grand dramatic framework is discernible," but only "through the awkward language and the naive ideas."[2] C. F. Tucker Brooke refers to "the artless and provincial makeshifts of guild performances and the yet ruder devices of the incipient morality."[3] More recently, Harold C. Gardiner in his *Mysteries' End* speaks of "their more sober and moving devotional aspects, which undoubtedly impressed the simple minds of the English craftsman and laborer and, indeed, of king and noble, too."[4] And in 1950 A. P. Rossiter sums up a half-century's scholarship with the statement, "From the literary point of view the workmanship is never far from crude and, in the older strata, insipid to a degree." By the "older strata" he seems to mean the Chester Plays which, as I have tried to show in earlier lectures, do not really deserve to be called older. Rossiter says also, "Probably most 'effects' were nearer children's improvisations than 'production.' "[5]

With this view I find it hard to sympathize; but I might be more disturbed by the solid unanimity of modern criticism of the mystery plays if I had not had the annual experience of reading the essays of Freshmen who patronize Chaucer. It is admittedly difficult for us who have reached the pinnacle of culture not to

look with contempt upon our ancestors who had neither Hollywood, soap opera, nor the atomic bomb. These are great
achievements which set our minds free for productive labours.
Besides, we have running water in our homes, upholstered furni-
ture, and all those time-saving mechanisms which have eaten up
our leisure. Still further, all of us can read and write, after a
fashion. But comforts and machinery are not an absolute
necessity of the higher life—unless the Greeks were less civilized
than we have been led to believe. A man may be well educated
though unlettered; learning by book is not the only way to learn.
Students in our classrooms seem content to sit hard, provided
there is some challenge in what they hear; and many of them
have actually been known to learn more by ear from men than
by eye from books. As a matter of fact, we tend to overestimate
the illiteracy of the Middle Ages; every monastery had its school,
and bailiffs and merchants kept records. I should be very glad to
debate—in the affirmative—that there was more real and genuine beauty surrounding the whole life and being of the ordinary
man of the Middle Ages than is to be found in a street-car and
assembly-line society. The men who dreamed cathedrals and
built them to centre every town; who made, for the wage of a
pound a year, less than a penny a day, stained-glass windows
such as have never been equalled and of such great beauty that
in modern times of war we have taken them out and catalogued
the thousands of pieces before burying them for safe-keeping;
who created the magnificent ceremonial and music of the Mass;
who could fill their churches with such carving and statuary as
the world would not lose; who could preserve for us the work
of Chaucer, Erasmus, and Holbein: such men were not necessarily childish or crude.

Moreover, we have seen that business men were under heavy
expense to keep the plays going. Business men in all ages have
prided themselves on knowing the value of money; yet we have

seen the Chester gildsmen, or their representatives who formed
the civic council, fight bitterly against the opposition of the new
Church to retain the privilege of heavy expenditure on mystery
plays. Still further, these plays had universal appeal and universal approval for more than two hundred years. If our ancestors were childish, why did they not tire sooner of their pro-
vincial makeshifts and childish improvisations? Let us not seek
escape in the naïve notion that two hundred years then was
somehow shorter than two hundred years now. Set it out in
panorama: we must travel almost from the Spanish Armada
back through the reign of Philip and Mary and the restoration
of the Church of Rome, back through Henry VIII and the Disestablishment, back through the dawn of the English Renaissance and the introduction of printing, back through the long
Wars of the Roses, past Agincourt, past the boy king whose
cousin in civil war drove him from the throne, past the Peasants'
Revolt, past Wycliffe and his preaching friars, and well into the
long reign of Edward III. During that immense period of swift
and violent change, the mystery plays held their own. For dramatic longevity their only rival is Shakespeare; and I take it
that the real duty of criticism is not to brush them aside as crude
and childish, but to ask what there was in them that could appeal
to sane and sensible men in a civilized country for more than
two hundred years.

When the scales have fallen from our eyes, we shall see at
once that the mystery plays had the advantage over all other
drama and over all literature except the Bible, Dante, Milton,
and a few minor authors, of the grandest, most sublime, and
most powerfully moving of all themes. When a theme is greater
than its handling, the effect is inevitably comic—like a clown
parading in clothes too large; but nobody has ever found the
mysteries unintentionally comic. They were saved from that
fate, I should say, by simple sincerity and good taste. And when

we call them crude, naïve, and undramatic, we are only express-
ing our own inability, or refusal, to see them as they actually
were. What we need is a faith that our ancestors were not silly;
we need also the auditory and visual imagination that will en-
able us to attend a performance, sitting cheek by jowl with
dignitaries of the Church or officials of the city, or rubbing
shoulders in the streets with men and women who had the same
appreciation of art in all its forms that we have—or perhaps an
appreciation not quite so dulled as ours has been by the clanking
machinery of modern life, or left so uncultivated as ours by the
absence of artistic objects around us.

One thing must be admitted: blank verse not yet having been
invented, and prose not yet having found her Dryden, the mystery plays had to struggle with the Procrustean requirements of
an unsuitable medium. Nor had Shakespeare yet enunciated his
great doctrine that "The play's the thing," or demonstrated that
poetry should be the handmaiden of drama, and not its mistress.
These were things that Shakespeare had to learn for himself;
and if even he could in his early days be confused on this issue,
we can hardly blame the common people for writing their plays
in verse—and sometimes, be it admitted, in verse at all costs. We
only continue their error, however, when we look for "literary"
qualities in the mystery plays. What we should look for in drama
is drama; and seeking it in the mysteries, we shall find.

We should look for the same things that we always look for in
the theatre: entertainment, beauty, representations of human
life, the power to grip and hold an audience, and—above all—
meaning or significance or, if I may say so, moral value.

And, in all fairness, there are certain things we should remember. One is that we may not have true witness to the mysteries
in the manuscripts which survive. All of the copies of the Chester Plays were made by late scribes who, often enough, did not
understand their exemplars, and who tried to make them intel-

ligible—with sad results. We should therefore keep in mind an apt remark of Sir E. K. Chambers: "Whoso would read the plays to-day must often go darkling."[6]

Perhaps we should bear in mind the mere possible itself. If the greatest dramatic genius of all time had had the task of working up the Biblical story into drama at the end of the fourteenth century, what could he have done? As I have said, there was no Shakespearean example for him to follow; so far as he knew, the theatre of the ancient world did not exist; the theatre of modern times did not exist; neither blank verse nor prose had yet been created as a vehicle of expression. What is to be expected? On the other hand, after the stage and the vehicle and the Elizabethans have been created and done their work, what is to be expected? Considering our possible, have we so much to glory in after 1623? Nobody has yet surpassed Shakespeare, our inheritance. Did the mystery plays—even on the basis of what I have already pointed out about them—fail to surpass their heritage? It is a nonsense question. On the ground of that relativity alone, without even considering what the intrinsic merits of the plays may be, we can say at once that the unanimous modern opinion that the mysteries are crude and childish is the teaching of false prophets.

Again, to take one element which is constant in the plays, let us think of the singing. We cannot suppose that the potentials of the human voice have improved a great deal in the last five hundred years, or that the happy mother singing about her housework in the Middle Ages did so in a voice much worse than those that now bleat at the modern housewife from the morning radio. Indeed, since there was no radio then, and since people had to create their own amusements, it is likely that the ordinary person had better skill of this sort then than the ordinary person has today; and along with that universality of skill, there was perhaps taste and appreciation in judging the accomplishments of others. The term "Merrie England" has no modern relevance: it is a phrase that fitted an England that was "a nest of singing birds" long ago. When the Angel sang "Gloria in excelsis," or Old Simeon, "Nunc dimittis," or Noah and his family within the Ark sang, "Save me, O God," when the angels at the Last Judgment choired, "Rejoice in the Lord" or "The Lord and Saviour of the World," we may be perfectly sure that the singing was as well worth hearing as most of that which we now pay dollars per seat to hear. Indeed, we may spend a wry moment in the thought that with all our modern superiority, the great hymns of the Church are still those of the Middle Ages.

Neither the musical heart nor the merry one need be unrealistic; and the people of the Middle Ages came to close grips with life in a way in which we, on the whole, do not. Among the people of the Western world there has never been in modern times anything like the Black Death. Seeking for comparison one must go to the dreadful scourges of the Far East or think of that Christian gift which our own superior civilization and culture dropped upon the Japanese at Hiroshima. It is said that in the great plague of 1348 only one house in Chester remained unvisited by the Angel of Death; and the owner of that house inscribed in great letters across the front, "The House of God's Providence." There were whole villages in England in which every man, woman, and child died of the plague. Time after time in their flourishing period, the Plays of Chester could not "go" because of the pestilence, and the bodies of the dead were carried in dump carts to great community graves beyond the walls. What would the people of those times think of the "modern realism" of sophomoric writers lapped in security and comfort and uncompromisingly facing life in the raw at second, third, or fourth hand? A peasant woman once said to such a sophisticate, "Ach, what do you know of life? Haf you effer been hungry?" For a great deal of modern literature our ancestors would

have had the contempt that we have for drugstore cowboys and
beardless men of the world.

It would, indeed, be easy to pull out of the Chester Mysteries
passages that would shock any modern audience out of their
seats—even an audience brought up on the suggestiveness of
Hollywood, the "raw meat" that offends Boston, and, perhaps,
such unrelieved filth as *Tobacco Road*. What would a modern
author do with such a subject as the Slaughter of the Innocents?
The writers of the Chester Plays had no desire to shock for the
sake of shocking, but simply wished to tell the truth. The difference is that they were much closer to the basic truths of life than
we are. They knew that, whoever gave the command to slaughter all male children under two years of age, the soldiers who
carried out the order were hardly likely to be gentlemen and
scholars, but such as Hitler found to man the concentration
camps. And they knew that women will not quietly allow their
babies to be murdered. How does one find out or prove that a
child under two years of age is male or female? The simple
naturalism of the mediaeval dramatist has both more freedom
and more honesty than much of our modern realism.

Let me turn away from that subject and remark that in the
Chester Slaughter of the Innocents there is one touch of the
grimmest dramatic irony. It was Herod who commanded the
slaughter of the children and, among the rest, Herod's own son
is slain. The Nurse has genuine touches of characterization.
When the child is slain, she cries out:

> Out! Out! Out! Out!
> You shall be hanged, all the rowt!
> Theues, be you neuer so stout,
>     Full fowle you haue done.
>
> This Child was taken to me
> To looke to: Theues, wo be ye!
> He was not myne, as you shall see,
>     He was the kinges sonne.

I shall tell whyle I may drye,
His child was slayne before myne eye.
Theues, ye shall be hanged hye,
   May I come to his hall.

But, or I go, haue thou one!
And thou another, Sir John!
For to the kinge I will anone,
   To playn uppon you all.

Thus, after laying about her with a will, this raging tigress ramps off to the King.

He rages also, but there is a final touch of irony in that the Slaughter of the Innocents was commanded in order to kill the child who threatened to become King of Judaea; and broken-hearted Herod has to admit that of all the children in the land his own was least likely to be spared:

He was right sicker in silk aray,
In gould, and pyrrye that was so gay,
They might well know by his aray,
   He was a kinges sonne.

While this play is before us, a few further remarks may not be amiss. After hearing of the death of his son, Herod goes on:

Alas! What the devill is this to mone  [mean]
Alas! My days be now done;
I wott I must dye soone,
   For damned I must be.

My legges rotten and my armes;
I haue done so many harmes,
That now I see of feendes swarmes
   From Hell cominge for me.

Presently he dies. The line, "My legges rotten and my armes" may recall to our minds that in what Sir Winston Churchill has called "the quaint account," he perished eaten by worms. It was not quaint to our ancestors: they had seen flesh turn black and rot time and again in the terrible visitations of the Black Death.

Herod dies, and a very lively and engaging Demon enters to drag him off; for, like the Elizabethans, the mediaeval dramatist had to get rid of "dead bodies":

> Warr, warr! for now unwarly wakes you woe!
> For I am swifter than is the doe.
> I am commen to fetch this lord you froe
>   In woe ever to dwell.
>
> And with this croked cambrock your backs shall I cloe,
> And all falce beleuers I burne in a low,
> That from the crowne of the head to the right toe,
>   I leave no wholl fell.
>
> From Lucifer, that lord, hither I am sent
> To fetch this kinges sowle here present,
> And to Hell bring him ther to be lent
>   Euer to lyve in woe.
>
> Ther fyre burnes bloe and brent;
> He shall be ther, this lord, verament;
> His place euermore therin is hent,
>   His body neuer to goe froe!

Like Shakespeare, the mediaeval dramatist could convert a handicap into an asset. The handicap, the difficulty, is the dead body of Herod. In disposing of it, he creates this lively Demon and drives home the lesson that the wages of sin is death.

As if the spectacle of a magnificent King, with a page-boy to hold up the train of his robes, being dragged off to Hell, were insufficient to emphasize the equality of all men under God, the Demon now turns to the audience with a warning to another class of sinners:

> No more shall you Tapstars, by my lewtye,
> That fills your measures falcly,
> Shall bear this lord Company,
>   They gett none other grace.

I will bring this into woe,
And come agayne and fetch moe,
As fast as ever I may go.
    Farewell and haue good day!

No doubt the Innkeepers once had a connection with this play.
However that may be, this lusty Demon has no sooner dragged
Herod off the stage than an angel appears to the Holy Family
and tells Joseph and Mary to return with the child Jesus into
Judaea. But it took Shakespeare years to learn the value of con-
trast in drama.

Time is telescoped in this play—as, indeed, it has to be in all
drama. But the material is there for a good production with the
grimmest reality, terrifying irony, demonic gusto, and, for contrast, the Angel who, before the Slaughter began, warned the
Holy Family to go forth into Egypt.

Let us turn back for a moment to that earlier scene. Leading
forth Mary, Joseph, and the child Jesus, the Angel says:

Come now furth in God's name!
I shall you sheild from all shame,
And you shall see, my leefe dame,
    A thing to your lykinge.

For Mahometis, both one and all,
That men of Egipt gods can call,
At your coming downe shall fall,
    When I begin to singe.

True enough, the stage direction reads: "Then they will go
forth, and the Angel will sing, 'Behold, the Lord will rise above
the clouds, and will enter into Egypt, and the images of Egypt
will fall down before the face of the Lord of Hosts,' and if it
can be done, let some statue or image fall." Certainly it could
be done! We cannot escape the conviction that our ancestors
knew the value of stage effects.

Though I began with the question of truth or reality in drama,

let us review what is to be found in the Slaughter of the Innocents so as to visualize one complete unit from the Chester Plays.
First of all, Herod appears, raging that the Magi have eluded
him. He calls for "petty Prat" his messenger, and sends him
after his "doughty and comely knightes." With this preparation,
we can easily imagine just how loathsome and foul his comely
knights will be. Having waked these slumbering beasts, petty
Prat brings Sir Grimbalde, Sir Launcherdepe, and Sir Wara-
drake to the King. They at first object to the commission: the
killing of infants is no fit task for such doughty men of war; in
the end, however, off they go. While they approach Bethlehem,
the Angel warns the Holy Family and leads them away; and as
he approaches Egypt with them, we see the images fall at the
sound of his song. Immediately we turn to the sharp, grim horror of the Slaughter itself, at the end of which the Nurse rushes
to scream at Herod that his son has been slain. Herod dies, and
the boisterous Demon fetches him off to Hell, with a promise to
return in the twinkling of an eye to carry away other sinners.
The Angel appears again to Joseph and Mary, saying:

> Now you be ready for to goe,
> Joseph and Mary also,
> Forsooth I will not depart you froe,
>   But help you from your foe.

> And I will make a melody,
> And singe here in your company,
> A word was sayd in prophesye
>   A thousand yeare agoe.

And the play ends with the Angel's song.

If that isn't drama, then in the name of all that's mysterious,
what is? Is it possible that Shakespeare is only drama because
we have *seen* him on the stage? Have we no imagination to present to the inward eye and ear that which we have not actually
beheld and heard? There have been in modern times some en-

chantingly beautiful motion pictures, and some with grim ele-
mental significance: I shudder to think what our imperceptive
mediaeval scholars would make of them if they were limited to
the written scenarios as, in a sense, we are limited when we read
mystery plays. Here, at any rate, in this many-faceted gem, in
this little play of the Slaughter of the Innocents, surely there is
God's plenty of contrast, of beauty and ugliness, of effective
staging, of vivid and memorable teaching of the word of God.
The scenes shift with the rapidity which we find elsewhere only
in ballads, but they build up into an impressive wholeness and
unity—and that in a bare 496 short lines. The play could be
produced today, or any day, with grim and beautiful and powerful effect, but not by producers who think our ancestors crude,
simple, and naïve, and not by actors who, like some I have heard
on the air, suspend their animation when they approach a
mediaeval Christmas play.

If, out of deference to modern proprieties, I have spared you
the naturalness of the lines spoken during the *mêlée* of women
and soldiers in the Slaughter of the Innocents, neither can I
quote from the Crucifixion lines which terribly impress upon the
mind the ugliness and horror of that spectacle. Our forefathers,
as I have said, lived at grips with nature and close to earth.
Every man, woman, and child in Chester had seen animals
slaughtered for food; they knew the details that express in beasts
the last extremes of pain and torment. Nay, they had seen
human animals hanged at the High Cross or burnt at the stake;
and our Lord, the Son of God, was also a human animal. When
they exhibited Him "tugged, lugged, all to-torn," they could do
so with such reality as makes the lines excessively painful reading, shattering to the soul, so that the play, when produced, must
have been one of the most terrible things ever seen on a stage.
I shall spare you details natural to our ancestors, and quote some

of the grisly joy of the soldiers as they bind the Lamb of God to
the Cross:

*Fourth Soldier:*    Fellows, will ye se
How sleight I will be,
This fyst or I flye,
    Here to make fast?

*First Soldier:*    Yea, but as mott I thee,
Short-armed is he:
To bring to this tree,
    It will not long last.

*Second Soldier:*    Ha! therefore care thou nought!
A sleight I haue sought:
Ropes must be brought
    To strean him with strength.

*Third Soldier:*    A rope, as behight,
You shall haue, vnbought.
Take here one well wrought,
    And draw him on length.

            *Tunc ligabunt Cordam ad sinistram
            manum quia dextra erat prius fixa.*

*Fourth Soldier:*    Draws, for your father kynne!
Whyle that I dryve in
This ilke iron pynne
    That, I dare lay, will last.

*First Soldier:*    As ever haue I wynne,
His arm is but a fynne!
Now dryves on, but dyn,
    And we shall draw fast.

            *Tunc tres trahent et quartus transfiget
            clavem.*

Lest the lines seem unintelligible to hearing, let me paraphrase them. The soldiers are binding our Lord to the Cross. The

Fourth Soldier says, "Look, you fellows—see what a good job
I can make of nailing down this fist!" The First replies, "Yeah,
but he's short-armed. How kin we nail his other arm to the
other side?" The Second puts in, "That's no trouble! We'll
stretch him." The Third produces a rope which they fasten to
the left hand of our Lord since the right is already nailed down.
The Fourth Soldier cries, "Haul, you fellows, while I drive in
the nail!" The First exclaims, "By cracky, his arm's only a fin!
Go ahead, drive in your nail while we haul on the rope." Then
the three go at it with a yo-heave-ho, stretching the arm while
the Fourth Soldier hammers in the nail. A similar grisly touch
of ghoulish inhuman glee comes when the Fourth Soldier cries,

> Fellows, will ye see
> How I haue stretcht His knee?
> Why prayse you not me
>    That haue so well done?

Is it possible that our forefathers who lived close not only to
life but to the Church knew nothing whatever about the basic
principles of art? Is it possible that they did not know that the
poignancy and holiness of that cry, "Father, forgive them, for
they know not what they do," would stand out in tragic and
terrible loveliness against such a revolting scene as this? Or did
they think an audience could, without being powerfully moved,
turn directly from these gleeful brutes and their ghoulish humour
to Mary the Mother of Jesus as she weeps:

> Alas, my love, my lyfe, my lee,
> Alas, mowrning now madds me.
> Alas, my bootë looke thou be,
>    Thy mother that thee bare!

> Thinke on my freut! I fosterd thee
> And gaue thee sucke vpon my knee;
> Vpon my payne haue thou pitty!
>    Thee faylës no power.

Alas, why ne were my lyfe forlorne?
To fynd my foodë me beforne
Tugged, lugged, all to-torne
　　With traytors now this tyde?

With neilës thrust, and crown of thorne,
Therfore I madd, both even and morne,
To see my birth that I haue borne
　　This bitter bale to byde.

But the way of modern criticism is to label such a piece a *planctus Mariae*, and having exhausted itself in that effort, to pay—blunted with community—no more attention to it. Well then, it is *not* a *planctus Mariae*, or not that merely—it has a powerful, and deeply moving dramatic effect.

The comic element in the Chester Plays, I have been trying to say, is always defensible on artistic grounds. Would that the same statement could be made of all our drama! It may be that this phenomenon is due to the Church under whose jurisdiction, as I have tried to show, the plays remained until 1531; and to the new Church whose gaze was stern. But elsewhere, we are told, similar plays are not primarily didactic and decorous, but violate their fundamental purpose. And here I can hardly do better than quote from Gayley:

The French mystery poets, while they develop, like the English, the comic quality of the shepherd scenes, introduce the drinking and dicing element *ad lib.*,—and sometimes the drabbing; they make, moreover, a specialty of the humour of deformity, a characteristic which appears nowhere in the English plays. The Germans, in their turn, elaborate a humour peculiar to themselves, —elephantine, primitive, and personal. They seem to get most fun out of reviling the idiosyncrasies of Jews, whose dress, appearance, manners, and speech they caricature—even introducing Jewish *dramatis personae* to sing gibberish, exploit cunning, and perform obscenities under the names of contemporary citizens of the hated race. In general a freer rein seems to have been given to the sacrilegious, grotesque, and obscene on the Continent than in England.[7]

The English plays, in short, and especially those of Chester, never got out of hand, never forgot their sacred mission.

If there is in these plays grim realism and tragic beauty, they are not without minor qualities of humour and local chit-chat of a sort always popular with audiences. For example, Octavian in the Nativity play, sending his messenger with orders to have the Jews numbered, offers him for reward the "highe horse besides Boughton." Boughton is a district outside one of the gates of Chester, and the "highe horse" is the gallows. The impudent messenger answers in kind that such a horse should be ridden by great lords "of your degree," and continues:

> They bene high in dignitie,
> And also high and swifte is he;
> Therefore that reverance takes yee,
>     My deare Lord, I you praye.

Similarly, when Cain is banished and condemned to be a "lurrell" (rogue or blackguard), he turns to the audience as the play closes and says:

> Now I goe, to all that I see
> I graunt the same gifte.

In the highest art there is a kind of simplicity, an element of the obvious to which we say, "Of course!" But before that element arrived, it was as distant from our thoughts as Aldebaran or Orion's sword. It is at this point that art and science meet, for the great discoveries of the scientific world have been things which seemed utterly obvious once they were pointed out. That quality of the simple, yet unexpected, undreamed-of inevitable I find in an unobtrusive stage direction of the Nativity play of Chester.

But first let me ask a question: The ox and ass of the sacred manger, where did they come from? Most of us will have supposed that they were always there! And why were they not cows or horses?

When Octavius Caesar issued his mandate that all the people of his dominions should be numbered and pay tribute, Joseph and Mary went from Nazareth to Bethlehem for this purpose, and Mary rode upon the ass. To provide tribute money, Joseph took the ox along. He says:

> An oxe I will take with me
> That there shall be sould.
>
> The silver of him, so mot I thee,
> Shall finde us in that city,
> And pay tribute for thee and me.

There follows the stage direction: "Then Joseph will bind the ox to the tail of the ass, and place Mary upon the ass." They are now ready to set out on their journey. But what a picture this is: Joseph, an old man on foot, leading the ass on which the young and lovely Mary rides, and the ox following behind tied to the tail of the ass! And that humble procession adds one more surprising, yet obvious touch to the most appealing story our ears have ever heard.

Similarly in the Shepherds Play, the four boys who serve the Shepherds approach the child Jesus in the manger:

*The First Boye*: Now to you, my fellowes, this doe I say:
For in this place, before I wende away,
Vnto yonder Child lett us goe pray,
As our masters haue done vs before.

*The Second Boye*: And of such goodis, as we haue here,
Lett us offer to this prince so dere
And to his Mother, that mayden clere,
That of her boddy hasse him borne.

*The First Boye*: Abyde, Sirres, I will go first to yonder king.

*The Second Boye*:    And I will goe next to that lording.

*The Third Boye*:    Then will I be the last of this offryng,
    This can I say, no more.

*The First Boye*:    Now, lord, for to geue thie have I no thing,
    Nother gould, siluer, broch, nor ring,
    Nor no rich robes meate for a king,
        That I haue here in store.

    But tho it lack a stoppell,
    Take thie here my well fayer botell,
    For it will hold a good pottell.
        In faith, I can geue thie no more.

*The Second Boye*:    Lord, I know that thou arte of this virgine
        borne,
    In full poore araye sitting on her arme.
    For to offer to thie I haue no skorne,
        All though thou be but a child.

    For jewells haue I non to geue thie,
    To mainteyne thie royall dignitie;
    But my hudd thou take it thie,
        As thou art god and man.

*The Third Boye*:    O, noble child of thee!
    Alas, what haue I for thee
    Saue onely my pipe?
        Ellis trulie no thing.

    Were I in the rockis or in,
    I could make this pipe
    That all the wood should ringe
        And quiver, as it were.

*The Fourth Boye*:    Now, child, all though thou be comon from
        God,
    And be God, thie self, in thie manhood,
    Yett I know that in thie childhood
        Thou wilt for sweete meat looke.

To pull downe peares, appells, and plomes,
Old Joseph shall not neede to hurt his
    thombes,
Because thou hast not plentie of cromes,
    I geue thie here my nvthocke.

Could anything be more obvious, more simple, more inescapable, or more beautifully appealing? *Of course* the Shepherds have boys, apprentices! Only, we had never thought of
them and never would have thought of them. And of course
the boys would worship the Child with the Shepherds; and of
course they would offer gifts. But what have they to offer? *They*
carry no gold, frankincense, and myrrh in their pockets. They
give what they are likely to have and to treasure: a bottle without a cork, in which, no doubt, the lad carries a refreshing drink
to the fields; the prized hood which protects from the bitter
wind; a willow whistle; and a nut-hook for pulling down apples,
pears, and plums. The virtue of a gift is that it should mean
something to the giver, include the element of sacrifice and
the element of love. No modern writer could possibly have
imagined that most obvious and simple scene: it has the true
mediaeval touch.

Nor could it have been written by Geoffrey Chaucer, our
greatest mediaeval English writer. He, it is true, does show us
the Widow's cottage, and he shows us a few other humble
characters; but he sees them, as we see them with him, from
the outside. The mystery author saw those shepherd boys from
the inside, and felt their reverence. Further, as Tiddy has
pointed out,[8] "in all the abundant realism of these plays [the
mysteries] there is certainly no realistic portrayal of a gentleman"—but to have failed to notice Chaucer's interest in gentility
is not to have read Chaucer. The world of the mystery plays is
a world utterly foreign to the courtly and learned poets. In the
mysteries you will find no tortured allegory, no three-ply dream

visions, no fragrant gardens of love and the rose, no women set on the sham pedestals—or whited sepulchres—of courtly love, no Dresden china maidens whose every feature from grey eyes to dainty feet is catalogued in unrealistic detail. But you will find men and women, coarse, robust, and real, like as we all are or ought to be, with our grumbling and humour, our normal confusions, tempers, and sins. The Virgin Mary herself is a sainted version of the nursing mother next door; she is neither Criseyde nor Queen Guenevere, but as simple and real and true and natural as the girl of eighteen across the way with her first baby. In the mysteries you will find no debates on love and courtly manners, on points of courtesy and gentility; their authors have no such sophistication; and the audience for whom they were written would take no delight in fine points of argument upon subjects to them trivial. The mystery plays, in short, are folk drama.[9]

Further, no matter how we may sweat our Freshmen through the Prologue to *The Canterbury Tales* and proclaim that here is a cross-section of English life in the Middle Ages, in reality the life of the Middle Ages hardly appears in Chaucer at all. What does appear is London and the courtly circle, their pre-possessions and interests, with an occasional glimpse of the passing procession of life seen from the sidewalk and brought back to amuse the Court. Among those glimpses there is one of Absolon playing Herod "upon a scaffold hie"—in itself evidence that Chaucer had not seen processional plays. Why, if Chaucer was so great a part of all that he had met in England, is there no single scrap of a mystery play from his gifted pen?

Indeed, why is it that up until this moment nobody has ever been able to give a name that would stick to any single author of a mystery play? True, Ritson long ago suggested that Lydgate may have written such plays, but we look in vain for evidence that he did.[10] What he may well have written is a royal entry or two, but that is a horse of a very different colour—if it is a horse at all. The name of Sir Gilbert Pilkington has been proposed as author of the Towneley Plays, but it has not stuck.[11] Chambers formerly believed that Randall Higden wrote the Chester Mysteries,[12] but has recanted.[13] I have myself advanced as the originator of the Chester Plays not a court poet, but a Carmelite monk, Sir Henry Francis. Not a single other name can be associated with any of the mystery plays of England, plays which at one time were the bloom of life itself in a hundred towns.

The truth is that the plays had no authors—or, to say the same thing otherwise, they had the same authors as the ballads[14]; and they require for their appreciation much the same taste as the ballads require. Crude the ballads are, if you will, and often enough their language breaks down; but they reach felicities which no sophisticated writer could achieve. One such bit is the line in the ballad of the Wife of Usher's Well: "The channering worm doth chide." Not even Shakespeare could have written that line. So it is with the mysteries: they are the product of folk artistry—and the folk *are* artists. Professional drama has its achievements and its glory; and so has that of the folk: "There is one glory of the sun, and another glory of the moon, and another of the stars: for one star differeth from another star in glory."

No doubt in the first instance some member of a church or monastery, some Henry Francis of this period or that, was requested to provide a play for this or the other gild of craftsmen. Then the gildsmen took it over, altering here, adding or deleting there, simplifying, intensifying, humourizing, bringing the artistic expression closer and closer to life as they knew it until in a play like that of the Towneley Shepherds there is a work of art such as no single author, labouring upon any single bank and shoal of time, could possibly have created. Even though official revisers from time to time trimmed up the plays, they still come to us encrusted with the living and thinking of real people, dwelling in real towns, experiencing plague and pestilence, rain and sunshine, revelry and tragedy, life, birth, marriage, child-bearing, and decrepitude through generation after generation of brief lives. So brief were those lives, with a life expectancy at birth of twenty-five years in the fourteenth century—as against sixty odd years now—that the promise of an Hereafter was immediate and important to them, and religion was their daily bread. Chaucer we are obliged by his artistry to know, Chaucer and Gower and Lydgate and the courtly romancers; but they are not all England, but one small corner only. There is another England that looms large and comparatively neglected in the ballads and mystery plays.[15]

This is an England clustered closely around the hospitable and all-inclusive Church. In it, every craft gild had its special altar. In it, the craftsmen maintained their sick in the only hospitals there were, their poor and destitute in the only homes for such persons the Middle Ages provided. In it, in the carvings of pillar and altar could be seen that sense of the homogeneity of all life from which we have now escaped. The birds of the air are no longer fellow creatures of ours in this twentieth century; the animals of the field are no longer our brothers. To us St. Valentine and St. Francis of Assisi are names out of fairy tales. It seems merely naïve to us to bring on the stage Balaam's Ass and let him speak in human words; and no man today would ever dream, as did the builders of Laon Cathedral, of placing high in the nave representations of the oxen that hauled the stone for that inspiring House of God. No modern artist would dream of depicting the whole human race rising from the penis of Adam as it may be seen in the crypt of Glasgow Cathedral. I have refrained from reading to you passages from the Chester Plays which would only seem to a modern audience coarse and shocking. But to our forefathers, close to earth and reality as they lived, these things came quite properly within the circle of life as they knew it—and, do not forget, down to 1538, and even thereafter, the Chester Plays were first performed before Church officials at St. Werburgh's. Between our mediaeval ancestors and ourselves many things have intervened—among others, an age when the word "leg" became vulgar and unmentionable; but if we wish really to understand mediaeval times, we shall do well to leave courtly circles occasionally behind and see life whole in the mystery plays. And the first thing we shall learn is that the religion of those times was a living thing which included all life.

There was room in religion even for fun, as for every other element of life. One of the merriest households whereof this world holds record was that of St. Thomas More who, nevertheless, wore a hair shirt next his skin. And Dante was never a truer mediaevalist than when he reserved a special corner in Hell for those who do not smile in the sunshine and the sweet air of Heaven. The nonsense of the Boy Bishop and the mock sermon in no way profaned the Holy of Holies, but could be enacted before the High Altar itself. In the play of the Towneley Shepherds, the very cradle which is used for riotous comedy and in which the stolen sheep is hidden, is used a few seconds later for the infant Jesus. In the same way, the raw, rude Shepherds at Chester doing their best to make out the words of the angelic song, "Gloria in excelsis Deo et in terra pax hominibus bonae voluntatis," represent something we cannot appreciate as our fathers did. To one Shepherd the first word was "glere," to another it was "glori," to a third, "glarum"; and they go on disputing about the word though none of them understands its meaning. I have often thought of them while listening to grand opera, and even to church choirs. Stop a moment: satire on the enunciation of singers is commonplace enough, but these Shep-

herds were not poking fun at the singing of a prima donna:
they were making hash of the song of an *angel!* And that song,
"Glory to God in the highest, and on earth peace," was the
most beautiful, the most enchanting, the most inspiring song
ever heard by the ears of man. That song alone, the first Christmas morning, announced the end of five thousand years of
slavery to sin and the beginning of a new era when salvation of
our souls became possible. The greatest tidings man has ever
heard, that this erring dust might really take on the image of
God and inherit eternal bliss, came to us in that angelic song.
And that was what the mediaeval dramatist with his rude
shepherds was burlesquing. For breath-taking, colossal im-
pudence the scene is without rival in drama. But in the Middle
Ages God himself had a sense of humour and fully appreciated
the absurd and ridiculous. Between that God and us, Puritanism has intervened and dissolved the merriment of Merrie England.

Merrie England it was, in spite of daily hardship and priva-
tion and terrible scourges such as modern man may imagine,
but cannot know. And this is the England you will find in the
mystery plays. It is an England with the gift of naturalness
which has rarely appeared in our literature since the Reformation; it is an England with artistic instincts of a high order; an
England with a deep sense of the homogeneity of man and beast
and fowl, of all living things; an England deeply devout, into
every moment of whose life religion entered as a living force; an
England merry in the sunshine, in the springtime, in the summer
festivals; an England whose sanity and wholesomeness and
balance ought to be an inspiration to all who come after.

Specifically, as I have said, the Chester Plays, as compared
with other cycles, never lose sight of their primary purpose. Perhaps a comparison can best be presented in the words of Tiddy[16]
as he compares the York, Chester, and Brome plays of Abraham
and Isaac:

In the Chester Play, where Isaac is represented as a child, his boyish fright and his simple affectionate prattle are almost unbearably moving and pathetic. In the York Play, where Isaac is a type of Christ and is represented as a man thirty years old, the pathos and dramatic value of the episode are swept away. In the Brome Play, on the other hand, this ecclesiastical bias is neglected and the scene is even finer than in the Chester cycle.

All of the cycles have, in the whole and in individual plays, their special excellences. With fewer plays than York or Towneley, the Chester cycle seems to have a greater unity; and it is guided, throughout the whole cycle from the Fall of Lucifer and the Creation of the World up to the Coming of Antichrist and Judgment Day, by a restraining logic. The result is that the multiplicity of individual plays does not confuse, but conveys a single overpowering impression of God's might and majesty, His justice, and His mercy.

I would not be taken to say that there are no crudenesses or gaucheries in the mystery plays, any more than I would make the same claim for Jonson or Shakespeare. One instance in the Betrayal of Christ is a sort of *Post hoc ergo propter hoc* in reverse. Peter threatens Malchus:

> Thy ear shall of, by Godes grace,
> Or thou passe from this place.

That is, we know that Peter clipped off the ear of Malchus; therefore we have him threaten to do so—and transform him, in the process, from a crude, flailing, angry man into the very butcher of a silk button, calling his shots in advance. And it is certainly unskilled workmanship that lets the characters of the plays step before us and say, "I am God," "I am Herod," etc. Yet Shakespeare's Richard III steps out alone on the stage to say, "I am a villain," and even Iago is not far from exemplifying the same device. But drama, like politics, is largely the art of the possible, and largely convention. Shakespeare could have managed *Othello* without the crudeness or the conventionality of permitting Iago to announce himself, but would the audience wait for him to do so? The possible is two hours' traffic of the stage. And Shakespeare himself, confronted with the task of a dozen Biblical plays to be staged on wagons during one day, might have done no better with them than Masefield has done with his modern adaptations of the mysteries.

If, then, we may believe that the mystery plays are genuinely dramatic in that they present conflict in abundance, as well as beauty and entertainment, in that they reveal life, and convey the deepest significance, we may now ask what they contributed to drama in general, and especially to the Elizabethans who remain the chief glory of our stage.

They contributed, first of all, as I have tried to show, the physical stage itself, a stage on wheels which could readily convert an inn-yard into a theatre, box office and all. And with that stage, they contributed the whole repertoire of stage apparatus and effects. As we have seen, Ophelia's grave is no new device; it is centuries old, the necessary hole or trap in the floor for the Devil's ascent into the world or for the sinners' descent into Hell. The curtained inner stage and the "discovery" so frequent in Elizabethan drama are equally ancient, as we learn from payments made for curtains and cords. On this point a stage direction in the Last Supper of *Ludus Coventriae* is quite explicit:

Crist enteryth in-to þe hous with his discipilis and ete þe paschal lomb and in þe mene tyme þe cownsel hous beforn-seyd xal sodeynly onclose schewying þe buschopys prestys and jewgys syttying in her Astat lyche as it were A convocacyone.

Many other examples could be given. Most of the Elizabethan stage effects have their ancestors in the mysteries; and, as I have said, Ariel flying about in *The Tempest* is only a vagrant angel from older days.[17]

No doubt the mysteries also established some characters which became part of the Elizabethan stock. The Vice of the moralities has often been pointed out as such a figure: he connects the mummers' plays, through mystery, morality, and interlude, and even classical adaptation, with the Elizabethan stage.[18] But swaggering Pistol must surely inherit some of the blood and characteristics of Herod, and the impertinent Fool must go back to the Garcio or Messenger of many mysteries. Such identifications might be questioned, for there are, after all, ancestors in classical drama and in the *Commedia dell' Arte*, and even in folklore, for many of the stock characters of the Elizabethans; but such matters as these, I leave, like Chaucer, to "divines"— or experts.

Only, there is one thing which definitely did not come to Elizabethan drama from the theatres of Greece and Rome, and that is the inextricable mixture of tragedy and comedy which Shelley called "an extension of the dramatic circle." It is because of this very extension that Shelley calls *King Lear* the greatest play ever written—and that tradition of mixed comedy and tragedy, as we have seen, is the mingled yarn of the mysteries, the very stuff of which they are woven.

Another mediaeval tradition so strong that it need only be mentioned is the tradition of music and song brought in at every possible moment to set the stage, create the scene, or inspire a mood. And still another element which did not derive from classical drama is the capricious freedom with which time and place are handled. Sir Harley Granville-Barker has said that the actors of Shakespeare "carry time and place with them as they move."[19] They do so because their predecessors had done so for hundreds of years. The mysteries also contributed to the tradition, sometimes unfortunate, of poetical drama. But their greatest gift to the glory of the stage under the Virgin Queen is twofold: they fostered a tradition of acting which put the professional actor through his apprenticeship; and they prepared an audience capable of rising to Shakespeare.

At some undetermined time between 1580 and 1595 there were in the town of Chester 410 householders assessed to provide armour in time of war.[20] This little town which could never, before 1600, have contained within its walls more than 5000 people, made, as I have tried to show, a genuinely significant contribution to drama, a contribution as yet unequalled by cities on this continent twenty and forty and a hundred times as large and prosperous. Considered as an achievement within the limits of the possible, the Chester Plays are great indeed.

# NOTES

OF THAT WHICH ONCE WAS GREAT

1. See C. M. Gayley, *Representative English Comedies*, New York: Macmillan, 1926, I, xlii.

2. Arnold Edinborough has said, "The mask was the court version of the partly danced, partly spoken folk plays . . . an indigenous English form, and not an importation from Europe as has so often been assumed." See "The Early Tudor Revels Office" (*Shakespeare Quarterly*, II (Jan., 1951), 19–25), p. 22.

3. I trust I do not here disregard the caution of Karl Young (*Drama of the Medieval Church*, Oxford: Clarendon Press, 1933, I, 85): "The Mass, then, has never been a drama, nor did it ever directly give rise to drama. The dramatic features of this service, along with those of the Canonical Office, and the symbolizing of virtually every sentence, gesture and physical accompaniment— these phenomena may have contributed suggestions as to the possibility of inventing drama, and may, indirectly have encouraged it; but the liturgy itself, in its ordinary observances, remained always merely worship." [S. CHAMBERS on the? – per ills from him?]

4. This theory of the origin of drama in the Western world follows the beaten path; but it should be added that Allardyce Nicoll argues cogently that "the earliest liturgical plays may . . . be regarded rather as simplifications of an already existing religious theatre" in Byzantium (*Masks, Mimes and Miracles*, New York: Harcourt Brace, 1931, pp. 209–13). He feels that it is quite likely that the mediaeval mimes "who wandered far and were known in many Courts should have returned from Byzantium with plots and scenes in their heads which might, because of their Scriptural character, placate the austere prelates who wished to banish all mimicry from men's eyes" (p. 213). Although Nicoll's thesis seems well documented, we have evidence that much the same development as that traditionally believed in for Western drama has taken place in the New World. See Sister Joseph Marie, *The Role of the*

109

*Church and the Folk in the Development of the Early Drama in New Mexico,* Philadelphia: University of Pennsylvania, 1947. The best proof that a thing could have happened in the past is that it has happened again.

5. For a good summary of this argument see R. Pascal, "On the Origins of the Liturgical Drama of the Middle Ages," *Modern Language Review,* XXXVI (1941), 369–87. Millett Henshaw in his excellent, indeed indispensable, "Survey of Studies in Medieval Drama" (*Progress of Medieval and Renaissance Studies in the United States and Canada,* Boulder, Colo., Aug., 1951, pp. 7–35), says (p. 9): "The current theory of the origin of liturgical drama still holds the field. The attempts of De Vito, Stumpfl, and Pascal to overthrow it are no more successful than that of Oscar Cargill."

6. See Karl Young, *Drama of the Medieval Church,* II, 399 ff.

7. Additional MS. 16179, a seventeenth-century MS. which copies Chester records, has (fol. 12$^r$ from a lost [?] Letter Book, 260) an order of December 18, 42 Elizabeth, that "No Brotherhood or Fraternity of Journeymen be Permitted in this Citty." The gilds were gilds of *masters,* employers of journeymen.

8. Karl Young, *Drama of the Medieval Church,* II, 421–2, says: "Even though the Roman hierarchy was essentially friendly to Church plays during the closing centuries of the Middle Ages, this period actually witnessed the gradual transference of religious drama from ecclesiastical to secular auspices. The change came about not through peremptory legislation, but, if we may judge by the results, through the natural desire of both playwright and audience for an increase in the scope of the performances, for an enrichment of content, and for the use of the vernacular.

"So long as the plays remained closely attached to the liturgy, they were restricted in all these respects, and were capable of causing embarrassment to all concerned. However useful they may have seemed as aids to instruction, they were, in the nature of the case, intrusions into the liturgical system, and could not be permitted to develop indefinitely. . . .

"Particularly important in the general dramatic expansion, no doubt, was the impulse toward increasing the worldly appeal of the plays through the comic element. Although the germs of comedy are present in several of the liturgical plays, the hearty development of these suggestions was possible only in secular surroundings. Even the friendly clerical opinions of the drama reviewed above disclose sufficient evidence of an ecclesiastical vigilance discouraging to an easy gaiety."

It is, of course, extremely difficult in this matter to avoid a *post hoc ergo propter hoc* argument. Young, it seems to me, makes the development a too consciously planned sort of thing. He assigns too great a role to a conscious playwright. I feel that the plays are due to much the same sort of authorship as the mediaeval ballads. Actually, there is no evidence to cover the point; and A. P. Rossiter, the latest writer on mediaeval drama, says (*English Drama from Early Times to the Elizabethans*, Hutchinson's University Library, 1950, p. 63), "How dramatics got into the hands of the craft guilds is unknown." For what speculation may be worth, I suggest that the awkwardness of the church as theatre, the imbalance of the Mass with large insertions, and the necessity of help towards the costs of production, as well as inability of the choir to supply all the actors needed, are the real reasons for moving the plays out of the church. This change, in turn, brings about the use of the vernacular, not because of a conscious desire of the playwrights to increase the scope of their plays and enrich their content, but because the gildsmen could not speak Latin.

9. The name Mystery Play has called forth some objections. Sir E. K. Chambers, for example, says (*English Literature at the Close of the Middle Ages*, Oxford: Clarendon Press, 1947, p. 16) that no English play was called a "Mystery" before 1744. That date would seem to offer a fair precedent; but the word *mystery* was common centuries earlier as referring to a craft or craft gild. Thus a civic record of Chester, dated October 25, 3 Edward VI: "Whereas this Citty is and long time before the Conquest of England hath been an entire and free Citty for all w^ch time it hath been used that no person Inhabiting therein should excersise any Mistery or Occupation unless he were admitted into the liberties of the said Citty . . . Order'd that henceforth no Person shall Excersise any Mistery or Occupation unless he be first made free of the same Occupation & Mistery upon forfeit of 20^s etc." (Additional MS. 16179, fol. 1^r, a seventeenth-century copy of Civic "Lib. B.") When there is plenty of authority for the word *mystery* in English, it would seem unnecessary to lump under the term *miracle* two quite different types of plays.

10. *Drama of the Medieval Church*, II, 199–224.

11. E. K. Chambers says (*The Mediaeval Stage*, Oxford University Press, 1903, II, 151): "The earliest notices of morals [i.e., morality plays] are found about the end of the fourteenth century, at a time when the influence of the *Roman de la Rose* and other widely popular works was bringing every department of literature under the sway of allegory. That the drama also should be touched with the spirit of the age was so inevitable as hardly to call for comment." I cannot believe that the moralities, any more than the mysteries, were literary in origin—and, for that matter, Chambers himself points out allegorical figures in the twelfth-century *Antichristus*, which precede in time even the earlier part of the *Roman de la Rose* by at least fifty years. The reference is to the Tegernsee *Antichristus* (text in Karl Young, *Drama of the Medieval Church*, II, 371) which has such figures as Ecclesia, Synagoga, Mercy, Justice, and Gentilitas. Chambers suggests also that the *danse macabre* may have had an influence upon religious drama (*Med. St.*, II, 153).

12. Text in Karl Young, II, 371.

13. *Med. St.*, II, 154.

14. The influence of mediaeval preaching is excellently presented in G. R. Owst, *Literature and Pulpit in Medieval England*, Cambridge University Press, 1933.

15. See Robert Withington, *English Pageantry*, Harvard University Press, 1918–20, I, 136, 141, etc.

16. With this view Gayley, *Representative English Comedies*, I, liv–lvii, disagreed. He felt that moralities, miracles, and mysteries were of simultaneous and contemporary growth. A. P. Rossiter, *English Drama from Early Times*, p. 80, says, "the first Morality was in existence by about 1378."

17. Chambers, *Med. St.*, II, 108–9.

18. For example, Bale's *King Johan*, dated 1536, has a contemptuous reference to monks, nuns, friars, etc., "in syde cotys wandryng, lyke most dysgysed players"; see ed. of J. H. P. Pafford and W. W. Greg, Malone Society Reprints, 1931, p. 4. On p. xxii these editors tell us of John Bale that "About 1537 when the violence of his religious opinions led to his expulsion from his living, he formed, under patronage of Cromwell, a company of actors to perform plays in favour of the reformed religion." This troupe must

have *travelled*. A. F. Pollard long ago pointed out (*Reign of Henry VII from Contemporary Sources*, London: Longman's Green, 1913–14, II, 227–32) payments by Henry VII to acting troupes.

19. Chambers, *Med. St.*, I, 182, says: "Jacob Grimm was inclined to find in them [village ceremonies] the first vague beginnings of the whole of modern drama. This is demonstrably wrong. Modern drama arose, by a fairly well defined line of evolution, from a three-fold source, the ecclesiastical liturgy, the farce of the mimes [descending from the decay of drama in the Roman world], the classical revivals of humanism. Folk-drama contributed but the tiniest rill to the mighty stream." I would shift the emphasis, and say that the sources were folk drama, liturgy, and classical drama, the latter contributing perhaps both underground through the mimes, and clearly in the work of the humanists. But the mimes certainly kept alive a tradition of *acting*.

20. "Beyond this [the year 533 A.D.], the Roman theatre has not been traced," says Chambers (*Med. St.*, I, 21); but drama must have outlived the theatre, and we know that mimes and joculatori persisted as wayside entertainers and entertainers on festal occasions, even within that universal Church which had condemned them. We know also that puppet shows go back continuously to Roman times and beyond (*ibid.*, II, 158). And it may well be questioned whether the interludes which I have mentioned as being introduced as comic relief during the performances of the moralities could not be traced back to ancient Rome. Certainly the *Interludum de Clerico et Puella* (or *Dame Siriz*), a thirteenth-century work (printed by Chambers, *ibid.*, App'x U), suggests a far more hoary antiquity than the date of 1475 which I have assigned above as that of the beginning of modern activity in this genre.

Shakespeare's little play of Pyramus and Thisbe, acted by craftsmen, it may be added, suggests a tradition of non-religious interludes performed by craft gilds—but a tradition of which we know nothing.

21. The full accounts have recently been printed by J. R. Beresford in the *Journal of the Chester and North Wales Architectural, Archaeological and Historic Society*, XXXVIII (1951), 95–172.

22. Edward Doby appears in other records of Chester. In 1585 Chester Cathedral paid "To Edward Dawby for xxi ffoote of new

glasse for the windows in the songe schoole at 7$^d$ the ffote . . . xv$^s$ ij$^d$." Again, "Paid to hym for mendynge the ould glasse in the same schoole iij$^d$." See the Ven. R. V. H. Burne, "Chester Cathedral in the Reigns of Mary and Elizabeth," *Journal of the Ch. & N. Wales A., A. & H. Soc.*, XXXVIII (1951), 59. Doby appears further in the same records on pp. 60, 67, 76. In 1572 (p. 67) £12 was spent repairing the windows of St. Oswald's, and Burne remarks that the Dean and Chapter must have been very lax, "for the windows must have been in a very bad state to require £12 spending on them all at once." I suggest that the large bill was necessary to replace Roman stained glass. Another Doby—Richard—was employed to mend windows at St. Mary-on-the-Hill, being paid 16$^s$ in 1549, and various amounts down to 1562. No doubt he also was really employed to deface images. See J. P. Earwaker, *The History of the Church and Parish of St. Mary-on-the-Hill, Chester*, ed. Rupert H. Morris, London: Love & Wyman, 1898, pp. 229, 231, etc. to 253.

23. J. E. Tiddy, *The Mummers' Play*, Oxford: Clarendon Press, 1923, pp. 91, 92.

24. Harley MS. 2125, fol. 39$^r$.

25. Chester Assembly Book, 1529–1624, fol. 88$^r$; Harley MS. 2150, fol. 128$^v$; Harley MS. 2105, fol. 64$^r$.

26. Additional MS. 29777; Harley MS. 2133, fol. 39$^r$; Daniel King, *Vale-Royal*, London, 1656, p. 194.

27. *Med. St.*, II, 356.

28. *Ibid.*, p. 151.

29. Additional MS. 29777 actually assigns the Triumph to 1563 in the mayoralty of Sir Lawrence Smith, but Sir Lawrence Smith was Mayor from November, 1563, to November, 1564. If the Triumph was performed during his mayoralty, it must have been at Midsummer, 1564. Additional MS. 29780 and Harley MS. 2133 also date the Triumph 1563, but Harley MS. 2125 has the correct date of 1564, which, as above, agrees with the Treasurer's Report.

30. P.R.O., Deputy Keeper's Report, no. XXXIX, Appendix I (Welsh Records, Calendar of the Recognizance Rolls of the Palatinate of Chester, III [Henry VIII-George IV]), p. 83, shows the appointment of William Crofton "as one of the serjeants-at-law in the county of Chester during pleasure," Feb. 20, 1571–2. The actual record may be seen in Chester Recognizance Roll

a/233, m. 1(2). Harley MS. 2002, fol. 198–9, has a copy of an undated legal complaint of William Crofton, "one of the Queenes ma^tie Seriantes and officer w^thin this Com. palatyne and Anne his wiffe late the wiffe of Raffe Aldersay late of this Cittie Alderman decessed" against John Stevenson alias Gybons concerning rent due to Anne for "one messuage and dyuerse shoppes and other tenamentes lyinge and beinge in thestgate streate of the said Cittie."

31. Harley MS. 2125, fol. 43^r.

32. The Chester Free Public Library has a modern manuscript by Thomas Hughes entitled, "Extracts from the Treasurers Accounts and the Chapter Books of the Dean and Chapter of Chester, Dating from the Erection of the See in 1541 to the year 1870." The Treasurers' Accounts are also used by the Ven. R. V. H. Burne, "Chester Cathedral." For the items cited above see p. 76.

33. Chambers, *Med. St.*, II, 186.

34. J. T. Murray, *English Dramatic Companies*, London: Constable, 1910, I, 314–16.

35. Chester Assembly Book, 1529–1624, fol. 246^v.

36. *Ibid.*, fol. 364^r. See also Rupert H. Morris, *Chester in the Plantagenet and Tudor Reigns*, Chester: G. R. Griffith, (?)1893, p. 353; also, Historical Manuscripts Commission, Report VIII, Appendix, p. 333.

37. Harley MS. 1994. This is a copy by Randle Holme of an expense roll of St. Werburgh's Abbey beginning 16 Henry VIII (1525). The item quoted is near the beginning of the roll and appears to belong to the year 1525.

38. F. Simpson, "The City Gilds of Chester" (*Journal of the Ch. & N. Wales A., A. & H. Soc.*, XVIII (1911), 98–203), p. 125.

TOWN AND GOWN

1. Rupert H. Morris, *Chester in the Plantagenet and Tudor Reigns*, Chester: G. R. Griffith, (?)1893, pp. 317–18 n.

2. E. K. Chambers, *The Mediaeval Stage* (Oxford University Press, 1903), II, 348 ff.

3. Morris, *Chester*, p. 317, dates this document 1532, but on p. 204 he says that William Newhall "succeeded in 1543" as Clerk of the Pentice. This erroneous date of 1543 arises from a confusion of

William Snead, Mayor *secundo tempore* in 1531–2, with William Snead, Junior, who became Mayor in 1543.

Chambers, *Med. St.*, II, 349 n., takes 1543 from Morris as the date of William Newhall's "first entre"; and therefore decides that the date of 1532 for the Proclamation must be an error. He says, "Oddly, Canon Morris's error was anticipated in a copy of the proclamation made on the fly-leaf of Harl. MS. 2013 of the plays (Deimling, 1) which states that it was 'made by Wm newall, Clarke of the pentice [in R]udio 24, H. 8.'"

4. Morris, *Chester*, p. 575, has found some Mayors preceding Arneway, but these were unknown to the sixteenth-century antiquaries.

5. Harley MS. 2150. For date see F. M. Salter, "The Banns of the Chester Plays" (*Review of English Studies*, XV (1939), 432–57; XVI, 1–17, 137–48), at XV, 450.

6. See F. M. Salter, "The Trial & Flagellation: A New Manuscript" (in *The Trial & Flagellation with Other Studies in the Chester Cycle*, ed. W. W. Greg, Malone Society Studies, 1935, pp. 1–73), p. 28.

7. In Harley MS. 2060, fol. 36$^r$, Randle Holme copies a deed of William de Bell and Agnes his wife, daughter of Robert Arneway. It is witnessed by Johanni Arneway, "tunc Majori Cestrie." Holme dates it 6 Edward I, i.e., 1278. Morris, *Chester*, pp. 575–6, has Arneway continuously Mayor from 1268 to 1277, but not in 1278. On fol. 57$^v$ of Harley 2060 Holme has another deed "about 2 E I"—i.e., 1274; and on fol. 58$^r$ still another, of the same date, both "testibus Johanne Arneway Majore" and others.

The death of Arneway is mentioned under the year 1278 in both *Annales Cestrienses* and *The Chronicle of St. Werburgh's*. Neither of these chronicles, both of which were contemporary with Arneway, the *Annales* closing with the year 1297, mentions mystery plays. Both chronicles have been edited by R. C. Christie for the Record Society of Lancashire and Cheshire.

8. *D.N.B.*

9. II, 352.

10. The following may be given as an example of the errors one may fall into by depending upon a sampling of the early Chester antiquaries: Arthur Brown, in "A Tradition of the Chester Plays," *London Mediaeval Studies*, II, Part I (1951), 68–72, finds that in

Additional MS. 29777 Arneway is given as Mayor in 1326–7, while Harley MS. 2013 lists him as Mayor in 1327 and 1328, and Harley MS. 1944 has him Mayor in 1328. Brown therefore feels that Chambers had no need to substitute Herneis for Arneway, since Arneway actually was Mayor at the very time needed by Chambers' theory of the date of origin of the Plays. He feels also, p. 72, "that the tradition linking the origin of the Chester cycle of miracle plays with John Arneway and Randulf Higden is a very strong one, and should not be lightly set aside in favour of largely unconfirmed material supplied by Morris."

Depending upon a few Chester antiquaries, the earliest of whom wrote more than three hundred years after the events he mentions, and all of whom were trying to reconcile irreconcilables, Brown has managed to get a remarkable number of shoes on the wrong feet. Sir John Arneway certainly died in 1278. The contemporary chroniclers say so (see note 7 above); and as the Abbey of St. Werburgh's benefited under his will, and as the chronicle was annual, we can be quite certain that the date is correct. As for Arneway and Higden, Brown is defending a position which Chambers himself, for good reasons, found untenable. The "largely unconfirmed material supplied by Morris" leaves me bewildered. Most of the information which Chambers first used came from Morris; he did not need, later, to set aside his theories "in favour of" any new material supplied by Morris. Morris was dead, and other scholars were at work. Morris has, it is true, many slips and inaccuracies; but not only what he says about Arneway, but everything else in his book is exceedingly well documented. His footnotes on Arneway, for example, cite contemporary deeds and agreements which seem, on the whole, to offer better confirmation than the unsupported statements of seventeenth-century antiquaries.

11. *English Literature at the Close of the Middle Ages*, Oxford: Clarendon Press, 1947, pp. 24–5.

12. *Med. St.*, II, 352.

13. George Ormerod, *The History of the County Palatine and City of Chester*, 2nd ed., by T. Helsby, London, 1882, I, 382.

14. W. H. Bliss and J. A. Tremlow, *Calendar of Entries in Papal Registers relating to Great Britain and Ireland*, P.R.O., 1902, IV, 273.

15. C. F. Tucker Brooke says (*The Tudor Drama*, New York:

Houghton Mifflin, 1911, p. 8): "There is very respectable evidence
for the belief that the Chester performances began as early as 1328,
and that the text presented in that year was prepared by no less a
writer than the famous Ranulph Higden, author of *Polychronicon*."
J. E. Tiddy (*The Mummers' Play*, Oxford: Clarendon Press, 1923)
speaks of "other cycles, which are somewhat later than the Chester,
and should probably be dated from 1360 onwards" (p. 100).
Allardyce Nicoll agrees with Chambers in general (*British Drama*,
London: Harrap, 1925, p. 25). C. M. Gayley in *Representative
English Comedies* (New York: Macmillan, 1926) speaks of "the
scriptural pageants presented . . . afterward by the civic authorities
and the several guilds when church plays had come to be acted
commonly in the streets, that is, after the reinstitution of the feast
of Corpus Christi in 1311 (I, xiii)." On p. xxiii he says, "A tradition, suspicious but not yet wholly discredited, assigns their composition [that of the Chester Plays] to the period 1267–76." George
R. Coffman in "A Plea for the Study of the Corpus Christi Plays
as Drama" (*Studies in Philology*, XXVI (1929), 411–24) says (p.
411): "During the first half of the fourteenth century there was
created in Northern England in connection with the institution of
the feast of Corpus Christi a new kind of literary composition, intended for stage presentation." A. F. Leach, in "Some English Plays
and Players, 1220–1548" (*An English Miscellany Presented to Dr.
Furnivall*, Oxford: Clarendon Press, 1901, pp. 205–34), follows
Chambers in substituting Herneis in 1328 for Sir John Arneway
(see p. 231). A. P. Rossiter (*English Drama from Early Times to
the Elizabethans*, Hutchinson's University Library, 1950) says that
the vernacular drama began in England "not much later" than
1304 (p. 52). On p. 66 he says, "The earliest [vernacular cycle]
in origin is Chester, dating from *c.* 1327."

 There are a few welcome cracks in this solid wall of unanimous
opinion. A. W. Pollard in his *English Miracle Plays, Moralities and
Interludes* (4th ed., Oxford: Clarendon Press, 1904, p. xxxvi) dates
the first composition of the Chester cycle about 1350, but without
evidence or argument. Miss Frances A. Foster, in her edition of the
*Stanzaic Life of Christ* (Early English Text Society, Original Series,
CLXVI (1926 for 1924), p. xliii), cautiously advanced the theory
which I have here made explicit, "Possibly there is some truth in
the statement of the 1544 bans [read *1540*], which connect the plays

with the name of Sir Henry Francis. If he was senior monk of St. Werburgh's Abbey from 1377 to 1382, his period of activity corresponds very well with what we can infer as to the date of the original cycle." She bases this suggestion on the fact that material for the Chester Plays was borrowed from the *Stanzaic Life of Christ* which must itself have been written between 1327 and 1370. In her "Was Gilbert Pilkington Author of the *Secunda Pastorum?*" (*PMLA*, XLIII (1928), 124–36), she says (p. 131): "The Chester cycle, the most homogeneous of the four, has sometimes been dated as early as 1327; but the relation of the vernacular source, the *Stanzaic Life of Christ*, to Higden's *Polychronicon* implies a later date, probably well within the second half of the century." I note also that Millett Henshaw in his "Survey of Studies in Medieval Drama" (*Progress of Medieval and Renaissance Studies in the United States and Canada*, Boulder, Colo., 1951, pp. 7–35) speaks of the Chester Plays as "dating from the middle of the fourteenth century" (p. 14).

16. A. F. Leach, "Some English Plays," etc., p. 209. Leach offers on pp. 206–7 a story from Beverley about a play of the Resurrection dated "about 1220." But it is a stationary performance in the churchyard that is described, certainly neither a craft play nor a craft cycle.

17. Lucy Toulmin Smith, *York Mystery Plays*, Oxford: Clarendon Press, 1885, p. xxxi. Chambers, *Med. St.*, II, 109.

18. Hardin Craig, *Two Coventry Corpus Christi Plays*, Early English Text Society, Extra Series, LXXXVII, xxiii; Chambers, *Med. St.*, II, 109.

19. One takes his courage in his hands, however, in speaking of dating any early English document by its language alone. As I have shown elsewhere ("John Skelton's Contribution to the English Language," *Transactions of the Royal Society of Canada*, Third Series, XXXIX (1945), Section II, 119–217), the *New English Dictionary* is quite unreliable as a guide to the dating of words— and there is, so far, little other help.

Chambers suggests, *Med. St.*, II, 130, that the *Ludus Filiorum Israelis* was part of a mystery cycle at Cambridge. There are two questions, however: (1) Was it not a Latin play? (2) Was it not produced by a religious, rather than a craft gild?

A passage from Robert Mannyng's *Handlyng Synne* (see *Robert* of Brunne's "*Handlyng Synne,*" ed. F. J. Furnivall, E.E.T.S., OS, CXIX, p. 155, ll. 4637 ff.) is frequently quoted as evidence of mystery plays in England as early as 1303:

> Hyt ys forbode hym, yn þe decre
> Myracles for to make or se;
> For, myracles ȝyf thou begynne,
> Hyt ys a gaderyng, a syght of synne.
> He may yn þe cherche þurghe þys resun
> Pley þe resurreccyun
>
> . . . . . . . . . . . . .
> . . . . . . . . . . . . .
>
> ȝif þou do hyt yn weyys or greuys
> A syght of synne truly hyt semys.

First of all, Mannyng does not mean by "myracles" what we mean by mysteries. He is translating directly from French, and the French word he translates is *representemente*. He evidently approves of the liturgical plays:

> He may yn þe cherche þurghe þys resun
> Pley þe resurreccyun.

What he condemns "in weyys or greuys" is obviously the same old miming and farce of lusores, joculatori, and histriones that called forth the ire of ecclesiasts all down through the Dark Ages. We may concede that liturgical plays existed in 1303 in England; but we need better evidence before believing that any single craft or mystery play existed there before the mid-fourteenth century at the earliest.

Allardyce Nicoll, who quotes Mannyng in his *British Drama,* pp. 24–5, adds: "The result of this prohibition was distinctly not that which was desired; it merely threw the drama into the hands of those people among whom it was to flourish luxuriantly. The town guilds took over the representation of the plays and carried on the tradition to the sixteenth century." Surely Nicoll is nodding here. It would have been a very foolhardy gild that dared in the Middle Ages to act in flat opposition to the will of Mother Church. But Nicoll makes a similar remark in 1947 in his *Development of the Theatre* (3rd ed., New York: Harcourt Brace, 1946), p. 63.

Finally, R. H. Robbins prints "An English Mystery Play Fragment ante 1300" in *Modern Language Notes,* LXV (1950), 30–5. The fragment consists of 22 lines in French followed by a paraphrase in English. In it good order is commanded in the name of the Emperor during a *ludus*. Spectators are not to converse loudly, and it must be possible for men to pass among them. No speakers' names are assigned. The piece could be a pronouncement at a feast or game, a fragment from a narrative poem, or almost anything; whatever it is, it is not *English*, but a French document followed by an English paraphrase. We shall need better evidence to prove that mystery plays existed in England before 1300.

20. *Med. St.*, II, 108.

21. Salter, "Banns," *RES*, XVI, 16.

22. Cf. C. F. Tucker Brooke, *The Tudor Drama*, p. 14; G. R. Coffman, "C. C. Plays as Drama," *SP*, XXVI, 412; Allardyce Nicoll, *British Drama*, pp. 24–5; etc.

23. Lucy Toulmin Smith, *York Mystery Plays*, p. xxix. Perhaps I may take the opportunity to correct a small error in Miss Smith's Introduction, p. xvi. The civic officials sought the opinion of Dean Hutton of York regarding their cycle in 1568. He replied, according to Miss Smith, "that it shuld not be plaid, ffor thoghe it was plawsible to [read *70*] yeares agoe, and wold now also of the ignorant sort be well lyked, yet now in this happie time of the gospell I know the learned will mislike it." The error of *to* for *70* makes some difference in the Dean's meaning, but it is now part of the modern tradition concerning the York Plays. See, for example, H. C. Gardiner, S.J., *Mysteries' End, an Investigation of the Last Days of the Mediaeval Religious Stage*, New Haven: Yale University Press, 1946, p. 73.

24. *English Drama from Early Times*, pp. 55–6.

25. Corroboration may be found in the fact that even in the sixteenth century the Abbey of St. Werburgh's, now Chester Cathedral, continued to make much of the players. To fortify and encourage them for the arduous duties of the day, the Cathedral in 1567 and 1573 bestowed upon them "a barell of bere . . . to make them to drinke." See Ven. R. V. H. Burne, "Chester Cathedral in the Reigns of Mary and Elizabeth," *Journal of the Chester & N. Wales A., A. & H. Society*, XXXVIII (1951), p. 61.

26. The stage direction in Noah's Flood, given above, "And first in some high place or in the clouds, if it can be done, God speaks, etc." suggests, in the first instance, the towering Abbey.

27. For this record see Salter, "Trial," pp. 7–8. This date is the

earliest for a firm reference to the Chester Plays; it pre-dates the earliest reference given by Chambers by forty years.

28. *English Literature*, p. 20.

29. This record is in the Mayor's Book, 1520–1, Chester Town Hall. Morris, *Chester*, p. 349 n., dates it 1520.

30. In "Banns," *RES*, XV, 452, I gave the earliest date for the Drapers as 1467–8. It should have been 1461.

31. As proved by a Pentice Court plea of debt in 2 Henry VI.

32. Undated Portmote Roll, Chester Town Hall. This entry is for 8 Henry VI, John Walssh, Mayor.

33. I.e.:

> Also the Taylers with trew Intent
> *Haue taken on them* verament
> The assencyon by one assent
> To bring it forth full right.

34. P.R.O., Deputy Keeper's Report, no. XXXVII, Appendix II (Welsh Records, Calendar of the Recognizance Rolls of the Palatinate of Chester, II [i Henry V–xxiv Henry VII]), p. 140. See also Chester Recognizance Roll, 2/144, 11–12 Edward IV, 1471–2, m. 7 (5).

35. See Harley MS. 2054, fol. 36ᵛ. Morris refers, *Chester*, p. 316, to this record and date, but says, p. 410, "Their first charter does not bear an earlier date than 11 Henry VII, 1495."

36. This matter is discussed in some detail in Salter, "Banns." I now feel obliged to withdraw some statements made in the "Banns" articles. The reason is that whereas I formerly accepted Chambers' estimate of the great antiquity of the Chester Plays, now I do not. Labouring under that misapprehension, I formerly took the existence of a gild charter as *prima facie* evidence that the gild had a play at the time the charter was granted. Now I do not. When seeking the protection of a charter, the gilds always brought in as much evidence as possible of their peculiar and burdensome obligations so as to show up the contrast between themselves and those pirates, freebooters, or interlopers against whom they sought protection. The plea that a gild had to maintain Corpus Christi lights and a pageant continued to appear in such applications for charters and renewals long after both the Corpus Christi festival and the mysteries had disappeared. I now feel that if a gild charter fails to mention a play, the gild had none.

The Tailors have a charter of 6 Henry V, 1418–19. It is printed in Morris, *Chester*, p. 412 n., but there dated 1491. In it there is not a word about their play. The Shoemakers claimed in Portmote in 1499 to have had a charter in 14 Edward I, i.e., 1285. They certainly did not produce a play then. When the Tanners in 1362 pleaded to the Black Prince for a charter and for protection against the Shoemakers, they made no reference to a play. I take it that if they had had one, they would certainly have mentioned it.

37. Fly leaf in Harley MS. 2104.

38. So, Additional MS. 29777.

39. *Mysteries' End, an Investigation of the Last Days of the Mediaeval Religious Stage*, New Haven: Yale University Press, 1946.

40. Morris, *Chester*, p. 304, from Lease Ledger, Chester Town Hall, fol. 28$^r$.

41. See Chester Assembly Book, 1529–1624; Morris, *Chester*, p. 315 n., dates this record 1567.

42. Harley MS. 2067, fols. 88$^v$, 51$^v$.

43. Harley MS. 2037, fol. 197$^r$.

44. This letter and the certificate in answer to it appear in Chester Assembly Book, 1529–1624, Chester Town Hall, fols. 164–5. Copies appear in Harley MS. 2173, in Morris, *Chester*, pp. 319–22, and in the Historical Manuscripts Commission, Report VIII, Appendix, p. 366.

45. The language of the latest Banns seems to suggest an indoor performance: "And if any disdaine [the Plays] then open is the doore That lett him in to heare." Thomas Pennant, *History of Wales* [London: 1778], I, 145, suggests that the Plays were performed in 1600. That date is attached to the late Banns. Whether Pennant had other evidence, I do not know.

46. Lucy Toulmin Smith, *York Mystery Plays*, p. xvi, shows with what anxiety the officials of York tried to alter their plays so as to make them acceptable to ecclesiastical authorities.

A DAY'S LABOUR

1. George Ormerod, *The History of the County Palatine and City of Chester*, 2nd ed., by T. Helsby, London, 1882, III, 443,

says, "Archdeacon Rogers, as appears from the list of rectors of Gawsworth, died 1595." The Ven. R. V. H. Burne, "Chester Cathedral in the Reigns of Mary and Elizabeth" (*Journal of the Chester and N. Wales A., A. & H. Society*, XXXVIII (1951), pp. 49–94), says (p. 75), with reference to *Sheaf*, 3rd ser., XXIX, 1, which I have not been able to check, that Rogers died in 1587. A copy of his will, dated June 17, 1580, may be seen in Harley MS. 2037, fol. 207ʳ.

2. *Chester in the Plantagenet and Tudor Reigns*, Chester: G. R. Griffith, (?)1893, p. 315.

3. *The Mediaeval Stage* (Oxford University Press, 1903), II, 348.

4. These materials from Harley MSS. 1944, 1948 are quoted in Morris, *Chester*, pp. 303–10; in F. J. Furnivall, *The Digby Plays* (Early English Text Society, Extra Series, LXX), p. xviii ff.; and in Chambers, *Med. St.*, II, 354–5.

5. C. F. Tucker Brooke, however, in *The Tudor Drama* (New York: Houghton Mifflin, 1911), p. 12, accepts Rogers literally. So does Allardyce Nicoll who in *British Drama* (London: Harrap, 1925), p. 25, speaks of Rogers as contemporary with the Plays. And, not to cite further examples, A. P. Rossiter, the latest in the tradition that stems from Chambers, is equally explicit (see *English Drama from Early Times to the Elizabethans*, Hutchinson's University Library, 1950, p. 63).

6. See *ante*, Lecture II, p. 46.

7. "Book Containing Fragments of Assembly Orders," Chester Town Hall; Morris, *Chester*, p. 317 n.

8. Morris, *Chester*, p. 306 n., referring to Harley MS. 2150, says: "Thus the Drapers paid viijᵈ rent for their 'caredge house nere to yᵉ Greye frere lane ende'; the Tailors ijˢ vjᵈ for theirs in Fleshmonger lane near Wolf's gate; the Shermen, in Northgate Street, iiijᵈ; the Smyths for a place to sett their carriage adjoining to the Shermen under the Walles nigh unto a towre called the 'Dilles Towre,' paid the Weavers the comparatively large sum of iiijˢ yearly." Four shillings would indeed have been a "comparatively large sum" if it had ever been paid; but it was not. The Smiths paid the City, not the Weavers, 4ᵈ. The Tailors paid the same amount, not 2/6.

9. "The Banns of the Chester Plays" (*Review of English Studies,*
XV (1939), 432–57; 1–17, 137–48), at XVI, 16.

10. See *post,* pp. 72, 74.

11. Harley MS. 2009, fol. 41ᵛ: "Sciant etc. R. Dutton Armiger
maior etc. concessimus ad feodi firmam Roberti Hill totam illam
edificium siue domum vocatam the Taylers Carriage howse jacen-
tem in parte Austriale cuiusdam venelle vocatae flesshmongers lane
adiacentem terram vocatam wolffes gate aut newgate modo in
tenuro Aldermannorum et seneschallorum Artis sutarium vestiarium infra dictam cuitatem continentem in longitudine 5 virgatas
regias et in latitudine 3 virgatas et dimidium habendum in per-
petuum Reddendi inde annuatim vt supra ijˢ vjᵈ ad festum St.
Michielis et Annuncionis beate Marie etc. Atturnasse etc. Tho
Thropp serviens ad Claudes etc. Dat. Cestr. 10 Aug. 16 Q. E." See
also Harley MS. 1996, fol. 263; and Morris, *Chester,* p. 306. Perhaps this document gives rise to Morris's error (see note 8 above)
regarding the rental paid by the Tailors.

12. J. E. T. Rogers in *Six Centuries of Work and Wages* (14th
ed., London: T. Fisher Unwin, 1919) says (p. 327) that in "the
fifteenth century and the first quarter of the sixteenth," "the wages
of the artizan . . . were generally, and through the year, about 6ᵈ
a day. Those of the agricultural labourer were about 4ᵈ." Rogers
estimates that a payment of 4ᵈ plus meat and drink would be worth
about 6ᵈ.

13. Harley MS. 2172, fol. 17ʳ: "16 Q. E. Rich dutton maior,
etc. grant in fee farme to Robᵗ hill Tayler the whole buildinge or
howse called the Taylers Carriage howse lyinge on the south pt to
a lane called ffleshmonger lane nere to the land called wolfes gate
or New gate now in tenure of the Aldermen & stewards cetus sutar'
vestiarium infra dictum Ciuitatem contayninge in length v yards
in bredth 3 yards & halph paying ijˢ vjᵈ at feasts St. Mich. & lady
day prouffe as before dated 10 Aug. 16 Q. Eliz. Tho Thropp ser-
gant ad lawes attorney to deliuer possession. Red lib. 8 in latyn."
The last statement is of course added by Holme.

14. See *post,* pp. 72–6.

15. Horses were used at Coventry. Hardin Craig, in *Two Coventry Corpus Christi Plays* (Early English Text Society, Extra Series,
LXXXVII), p. 85, lists payments for "horssing of the padgeant"

and "for ij cords for the draught of the paygaunt." In the pages following he prints many references to "driving" the pageant. At Chester seven or eight men would have had great difficulty getting even a light wagon up the hill from the Roodee.

16. Copies of these accounts appear in Harley MS. 2054, fols. 13ᵛ–21ʳ.

17. The Painters' accounts for the latter part of the sixteenth century are in the possession of the modern Painters' gild of Chester.

18. *English Literature at the Close of the Middle Ages* (Oxford: Clarendon Press, 1947), p. 19.

19. See Lecture I, note 22. It is true that the Painters in 1575 paid "rychard dobye for goynge one the styltes at the barres rydenge vjᵈ," and for the same service on Midsummer Eve; but there would be no "goynge one the styltes" at the Whitsun plays.

20. Hardin Craig, *Two Coventry Plays*, pp. 99, 101, etc.

21. *Ibid.*, p. 89.

22. O. Waterhouse, *The Non-Cycle Mystery Plays*, Early English Text Society, Extra Series, CIV, xxxii; Chambers, *Med. St.*, II, 388.

23. Scholarship in general, however, from the time of Thomas Sharpe and his *Dissertation on the Pageants . . . at Coventry*, 1825, down to the present has accepted the open stage of Rogers for all the mysteries of England. Thus, for a sampling, C. F. Tucker Brooke, *Tudor Drama*, p. 10; Katherine Lee Bates, *The English Religious Drama* (New York: Macmillan, 1917, first printed 1893), quotes, p. 41, from the *Breviarye*, and on p. 43 speaks of "the English scaffold presenting but one open stage, with the story below curtained off as a green room." Most surprising of all, Allardyce Nicoll in his *Masks, Mimes and Miracles* (New York: Harcourt Brace, 1931) has many illustrations of stages of all sorts, not one of which is without a roof, yet accepts (p. 203) Rogers' open stage.

24. Chambers, *Med. St.*, II, 346.

25. Nicoll, *Masks*, p. 35.

26. As the Painters had the carriage the first day, they could adapt it to their needs in advance.

27. The Smiths' accounts are to be found in Harley MS. 2054 as copied by Randle Holme.

28. Canon Morris had access to these accounts and distributes them in his *Chester*. The letter *þ* in some sixteenth-century hands

resembles a modern *x*, and vice versa. Canon Morris read *axeyll tre* as *apeyll tre* (p. 305). This error has been copied by Chambers and other scholars; and M. Lyle Spencer in his *Corpus Christi Pageants in England* (New York: Baker & Taylor, 1911) says (p. 116), "Two apple-trees are clamped to the floor of the pageant to represent the country between Bethlehem and Jerusalem" in the Chester Smiths Play of the Purification. S. F. Crocker carries over this bit of stage scenery in "The Production of the Chester Plays" (*West Virginia Bulletin*, series 37, no. 4 (1), 1936), p. 77. Crocker's article does not really deal with production, but lists an amazing number of properties required for production of the series as a whole.

I believe a similar error of Thomas Sharpe's has been taken over by Hardin Craig, *Two Coventry Plays*, pp. 93, 97. On p. 93 the entry is simply, "apple tree"; but on p. 97 an item reads, "it. pd for a pece of tymber for an apeltrie ij$^s$ iij$^d$." Sharpe notes: "Adam and Eve, though not particularized in the list of performers in the cappers' pageant (in consequence probably of these parts being taken by persons who had played other characters in an earlier portion of the pageant) were nevertheless indispensable requisites, and the introduction of this appropriate and distinguishing symbol [the apple tree] is thus readily accounted for." But Craig shows, pp. xiv–xviii, that there never was any Old Testament material in the Coventry plays! The simple misreading of *x* as *p* seems to have far-reaching consequences.

29. Allardyce Nicoll says in *British Drama*, p. 27, "The actors in these pieces were all amateurs—members of the various companies who for a time put aside their labour to perform in the sacred mysteries." In his *Masks*, pp. 193–4, he seems cautiously and guardedly to favour a view that "the mimes and the *jongleurs* were called in to aid the amateur actors," because "the boasting tyrant [e.g., Herod], the jealous husband [e.g., Joseph], the shrewish wife [e.g., Mrs. Noah], the comic Devil with his canvas club and his warts [not to be found in the Chester Plays, although Nicoll seems to think he can be]—all these have their prototypes in the mimic theatre." In his *Development of the Theatre* (3rd ed., New York: Harcourt Brace, 1946), p. 76, he seems to return to his earlier view: "The gilds, having taken over the management of the cycles, provided the actors from among their own members. Gen-

erally these actors were paid a small fee. At Coventry one man received three shillings and fourpence for 'pleayng God,' etc." But 3/4 is not a small fee. Having received it, "God" could go fishin' for a month!

A GREAT RECKONING

1. *History of English Literature*, II (trans. by W. C. Robinson), 306.

2. *The English Religious Drama* (New York: Macmillan, 1917, first printed 1893), p. 181. It is fair to add that Miss Bates has written in eloquent terms of the "grand dramatic framework" and "mighty range."

3. *The Tudor Drama*, New York: Houghton Mifflin, 1911, p. 1.

4. *Mysteries' End, an Investigation of the Last Days of the Mediaeval Religious Stage*, New Haven: Yale University Press, 1946, p. 3.

5. *English Drama from Early Times to the Elizabethans*, Hutchinson's University Library, 1950, pp. 66, 63–4. Allardyce Nicoll seems self-contradictory. In his *British Drama* (London: Harrap, 1925) he says, p. 26: "Crude spectacular effects must have been aimed at. . . . As a general rule, however, the plays must have been acted without scenery, or with scenery of a most crude kind." But in 1931 he says in his *Masks, Mimes and Miracles* (New York: Harcourt Brace), p. 206, "No conception of the medieval theatre could be falser than that which pictures it as a primitive and simple thing." The difficulty is that most of his illustrations for the latter book are drawn from France and the Continent.

6. *English Literature at the Close of the Middle Ages*, Oxford: Clarendon Press, 1947, p. 21.

7. C. M. Gayley, *Representative English Comedies*, New York: Macmillan, 1926, I, xxxvi.

8. J. E. Tiddy, *The Mummers' Play*, Oxford: Clarendon Press, 1923, p. 97.

9. Tiddy has made this point before me: *ibid.*, p. 98.

10. E. K. Chambers, *The Mediaeval Stage*, Oxford University Press, 1903, II, 145; Sir E. K. Chambers, *English Literature*, p. 49.

11. O. Cargill, "The Authorship of the *Secunda Pastorum*,"

*PMLA*, XLI (1926), 810–31. See, in reply, Miss Frances A. Foster, "Was Gilbert Pilkington Author of the *Secunda Pastorum?*" *PMLA*, XLIII (1928), 124–36.

12. *Med. St.*, II, 145.

13. *English Literature*, p. 26.

14. A. W. Pollard, *English Miracle Plays, Moralities and Interludes* (4th ed., Oxford: Clarendon Press, 1904), says, p. xxx, "Each cycle as it has come down to us must be regarded rather as an organic growth than as the work of a single author." And Tiddy says, *The Mummers' Play*, pp. 98–9, that like ballads, the Chester Plays, especially Abraham and Isaac, are "as nearly free from self-consciousness as drama can be: like the finest ballads it [Abraham and Isaac] is bare and severely simple, leaving all possible scope to the imagination."

15. Against the folk authorship of mysteries Rossiter argues (*English Drama from Early Times*, p. 51) that the cycles *selected* from the Biblical story characters and incidents to suit a didactic purpose. "The vast plot," he says, "had no more use for Samuel or David than for those very dramatic persons Jezebel and Joab. It was controlled by a logic which was theologic; and it is this consideration which makes nonsense of the opinions of Professor Allardyce Nicoll and others who make the medieval plays 'distinctively the creation of the common people.' " One may agree that the purpose and logic of the plays was theological; they were, nevertheless, the creation of the common folk, of common folk in Holy Orders working together with common folk in leather and mufti.

16. *The Mummers' Play*, p. 95.

17. J. Q. Adams, "Some Notes on *Hamlet*" (*Modern Language Notes*, XXVIII (1913), 39–42), p. 40, points out that Hamlet moves to the four corners of the stage seeking a place to take the oaths of his friends without interruption (I, v, 148–82), and that his predecessor in this "stage business" is Balaam in Chester Play V.

18. Allardyce Nicoll, *British Drama*, p. 48, says, "The Vice has already been found in the mystery plays; he becomes an established figure in the morality. His sense of fun, his rascality, his quips, and his jests made him a stock figure, and it is no mere fancy that finds him under the guise of Feste and Touchstone at the close of the sixteenth century."

19. *Prefaces to Shakespeare* (First Series, London: Sidgwick &

Jackson, 1927), p. xxiii. Katherine Lee Bates, *The English Religious Drama*, p. 183, asks, "Was not England reared upon dramas that embraced heaven, earth, and hell within their limits, that encompassed all of time that had been and yet should be? What did it matter, after that, if Perdita and Miranda grew from babyhood to womanhood in a single afternoon, or the scene in the Globe playhouse was shifted back and forth between pre-Christian Britain and Renascence Italy?"

20. Rupert H. Morris, *Chester in the Plantagenet and Tudor Reigns*, Chester: G. R. Griffith, (?) 1893, p. 78. J. E. T. Rogers, *Six Centuries of Work and Wages* (14th ed., London: T. Fisher Unwin, 1919), p. 117, reckons that in 1377 only London, York, Bristol, Coventry, and Norwich had populations over 5000.

# INDEX

[In the following Index all references to individual plays of the Chester cycle are grouped, without cross-reference, under the heading, Chester Plays. References to Chester craft gilds are similarly listed under Chester Craft Gilds; and all notices of places and things in Chester (such as St. Werburgh's Abbey and the Roodee) will be found under Chester.]